Praise For *Unleashing Team Potential*

"A charmingly written, humorous view of the challenges and opportunities for management. Wittingly using lessons from our canine friends, the book provides lessons and observations that will undoubtedly help managers think about how they interact with others and more importantly how they can facilitate interactions for positive outcomes."
Alastair JS Summerlee LLD, PhD, BSc, BVSc, MRCVS, President and Vice-Chancellor, University of Guelph

"Unleashing Team Potential" is an entertaining and enjoyable read that reinforces important skills to enable managers to be conscious and better communicators."
Amy Kendall, Chair, School of Business and Hospitality.
Conestoga College, Institute of Technology and Advanced Learning

"Sylvia Plester-Silk deftly launches the book's chapters from lessons learned from her canine companions, outlining practical applications of team-building principles. Whether suggesting we be inquisitive without being fearful, base feedback on observation rather than assumption or reserve "no" for emergencies only, Sylvia draws on her own experiences as a management consultant to help us unleash our team's potential."
Harold Taylor, author of *Making Time Work for You*

"Through a playful approach, incorporating canine capers that exemplify the innate wisdom of the dog, Sylvia offers a fresh perspective to ways people can work together to "unleash" the fullest potential within teams. Whether a manager, aspiring manager, or team player, this is an entertaining and relevant read. *Unleashing Team Potential* provides practical skills and techniques that, when put to action, will lead to more enlightened ways of understanding and relating to others – in the workplace and beyond. If you want to enhance and facilitate the social capital in your organization, this is a must-read. Candid, thoughtful – absolutely delightful!"
Debbie Stoewen, DVM, MSW, PhD, Director of Veterinary Services, RSA Canada

Unleashing Team Potential:

Lessons for Managers from My Canine Friends

Sylvia Plester-Silk

ISBN 978-0-9920131-0-3

Printed in Canada

Cover image of brown leather leash supplied by iStockphoto/Thinkstock

FIN 26 07 13

Library and Archives Canada Cataloguing in Publication

Plester-Silk, Sylvia, 1964-, author
        Unleashing team potential : lessons for managers from my canine friends / Sylvia Plester-Silk.

ISBN 978-0-9920131-0-3 (pbk.)

        1. Teams in the workplace--Management. 2. Leadership.
3. Motivation (Psychology). 4. Dogs--Behavior--Anecdotes. I. Title.

HD66.P54 2013   658.4'022   C2013-904517-1

A million thanks to those who made possible my journey to published author! Whether it was coaching me through the writing process, inviting me to book club, supporting me through challenges, giving honest feedback, or celebrating the wins – I am eternally grateful. Cheers to my friends at CAPS (Canadian Association of Professional Speakers) who believed in my vision and held me accountable – you are an incredible group of people!

I am forever indebted to my incredible editing team – Kathryn Dean and my dear friend Marcia Nelson Pedde.

And to my fellow dog lovers who are so much a part of this journey – I am so appreciative.

Thanks to my husband, Mark, for his endless support, and to Josee who taught me so much.

With heartfelt gratitude,
Sylvia

Contents

Introduction ix

Ourselves

1 Body Language: What We Say without Really Saying It 1

2 Feedback: Making Sure You're Heard 7

3 Curiosity 15

4 Positive Focus: The "Dreaded Three" 23

5 Conflict 31

6 Self-Confidence versus Ego 39

7 Crate Restrictions: Self-Limiting Behaviours 47

8 Outdated Behaviour: Making Critical Changes 53

Our Leadership

9 How to Play with the Big Dogs 61

10 Alpha Dog Leadership..69

11 Achieving a Common Goal with Strategy 75

12 To Leash or Not to Leash? 83

13 Treats and Employee Appreciation 89

14 Inspiring Growth and Development 95

Our Teams

15 Competition versus Cooperation 103

16 Using the Resources on Your Team..111

17 Loyalty 117

18 Shadows: Overcoming Distractions 125

19 Pylons Gone Bad: Fun and Work 131

Our Deeper Issues

20 Bullying: Dogs against Cats 139

21 Burnout..147

22 Mental Illness in the Workplace...155

23 Employees' Hunches 163

24 Manager's Intuition 169

The Final Bark...177

Introduction

When my husband and I brought a bouncy black Lab cross into our lives, we got more than we expected. Josee has given us hours and days of fun as well as a crateful of challenges. But I didn't know she'd also teach me lessons about human interactions—including team dynamics. That was a gift, since the sole purpose of my consulting business, On Purpose Consulting.ca, is to help businesses understand and learn from the interpersonal dynamics that happen in teams. Her life also dovetailed with my 20 years of experience as a therapist. In that work, I was honoured by the honest and deep sharing of my clients, and although that was a different context, Josee's interactions with her canine friends and with humans touched on some of the matters of the heart, mind, and soul that my clients and I discovered. To write this book, I've combined three passions: my work with businesses, helping them improve their team dynamics; my experience as a therapist; and my lifelong love of dogs.

Although I've written this volume for managers and supervisors, it is also meant to benefit anyone in their work and personal lives. In the first three sections—Ourselves, Our Leadership, and Our Teams—I've presented anecdotes, case studies, detailed advice, and questions to review about topics such as body language, embracing change, and dealing with conflict. Other chapters describe issues that affect teams, achieving a common goal, leadership, and competition versus cooperation. In the final section—Our Deeper Issues—I deal with burnout and intuition, among other subjects. All the chapters are designed to help you become emotionally intelligent, skilled communicators and great team leaders.

Historically, dogs exist as part of a pack. By reading about the issues in *Unleashing Team Potential* and applying the techniques I've described, you'll not only help your team members survive, you'll improve their productivity and well-being, and you'll see them thrive.

Sylvia Plester-Silk
Guelph, Ontario
April 2013

~ 1 ~

Body Language:
What We Say without Really Saying It

Duke's body language was always consistent with his message. Whether he was feeling proud, happy, or angry, there was no mistaking his intent.

When my husband, Mark, and I purchased our first house, we adopted a small black Labrador from an animal shelter. It was a beautiful afternoon in May when I picked Duke up and brought him home, and that evening, Mark and I took him for a walk. As we strolled together up the sidewalk in our small town, I looked down at Duke. He was strutting along, holding his head very high—as if he was the most important dog in the world and he was showing off his new people. That's why we called him "Duke"—because of his royal bearing.

We never knew Duke's exact age or breed, but he was a kind, loving dog, and he was especially devoted to me. Our new canine loved to walk, run, and play in a nearby field. He also liked to cuddle.

A few months later, it was vacation time. Mark and I were on a tight budget with a new home, so we had to be creative about taking a holiday that would require us to kennel Duke. To save money, we decided to ask my sister, Bonnie, to keep him for the week. She was happy to do so. Bonnie lived in a community near a lake with a large, grassed yard, where Duke could play with my young niece, Krysta, and her friends. Knowing he would be well cared for, Mark and I left on our vacation.

After our week away, Mark and I returned to pick Duke up. I'd missed him terribly, and I was confident that he would feel the same and run into my arms with excitement the moment he saw me. As we drove up the driveway, Bonnie, Krysta, and Duke came out the front door. While the human elements came up and gave me hugs, Duke was not forthcoming. He sat down on the grass with his back to me, facing my sister. Through his body language, he was informing me that he was angry with me! In fact, he continued to communicate clearly that my decision to leave him had been unacceptable. Duke didn't even want to go into the truck to come home. He got on board only with the help of some treats. Perhaps he'd actually decided to remain with his new family, because, after all, they played with him and took him swimming with Krysta and her friends every day. Duke was a clear and concise communicator, and his body language was always consistent with his message. Whether he was feeling proud, happy, or angry, there was no mistaking his intent.

In human communication, body language is equally powerful. The reptilian part of the brain pays more attention to non-verbal cues and tone of voice than to the actual words we use, and this triggers unconscious reactions. As a new supervisor or manager, your employees will respond to you not only on the conscious level, but also on the unconscious, body-language level. And since you get only one chance to make your first impression, it's vital to convey a positive message through your body language in order to be accepted as leader.

I once worked at a local college doing "standardized patient work." For this job, I played the role of a patient, "Jane," so that nursing students could have real-life interactions and then receive feedback about how the "patient" experienced the nurse's assistance. During one interview, the student moved the palm of her hand towards me and then down. Her words and intonation were fairly neutral, yet it was the body language that seemed to have the greatest impact on me. As Jane, I felt patronized—as if the nursing student was dismissing what I was telling her.

When we discussed this later, the student said she'd been trying to control her natural hand gestures in order to appear "more professional." As the class engaged in this conversation, she began to relax and use hand gestures where her palm was angled towards me, and I told her how this gesture helped me feel that I could trust her more. Even knowing as much about communication as I do, I was surprised to discover the power of such a small change in body language.

For successful conversations, it is essential to be aware of your body language. Like the student who was actively working on her hand gestures, you can learn by reflecting on your interactions with a co-worker. Notice what your common gestures are.

- How do you stand? Do you lean on something? Do you stand up straight?
- When sitting, do you sit up straight or do you slouch?
- What do you do with your hands? Do you hold them in front of you or behind you? Do you cover your mouth with them? Are your palms opened or closed?
- What does your face show your listeners? Do you smile or do you frown?
- Do you maintain eye contact, do you stare, or do you avoid eye contact?
- What does your tone of voice convey? Are your words calm or are they sharp and demanding?

The reptilian part of the human brain, which governs human reaction to body language, is also the part that tells us to fight or flee. Since these responses are unconscious, we often don't realize what has put us off during a conversation, just as Jane didn't know at first that it was the nursing student's hand gesture that triggered her reaction of distrust.

When we stand up straight, we are sending a message that we are confident and interested in the conversation. Slouching is likely to be interpreted as disinterest or boredom, and it may cause your listener to feel dismissed and unimportant. Do you stand *over* people who are sitting down? Do you crouch so you're at the same eye level as the other person? Both of these gestures reveal information about your intentions and can be read as overpowering or submissive, respectively.

Hand gestures can build or break trust. A few short centuries ago, people wielded swords and other hand weapons to protect themselves. If one person met another and extended an open palm, the other person would be assured that the first one didn't intend any harm. In fact, that is how the common handshake came into being. It indicated that neither person was bearing arms and that the interaction would be friendly. Hand gestures are often interpreted differently, depending on situations and cultures. If you were chatting with someone and gave the thumbs-up sign, your gesture would mean that you supported or agreed with what was being said. Conversely, if you were scuba diving and used the thumbs-up gesture, you would be saying that you were moving towards the surface, often because of a problem.

Your facial expressions will also show individuals whether you're being straightforward or whether you're hiding something. Rolling your eyes is dismissive. Holding your hand in front of your mouth frequently suggests that you are hiding something. In fact, facial expressions are so revealing that Canadian customs officers take a course specific to reading facial expressions so they can determine whether a person is being honest, is lying, or is withholding information from them.

To develop self-awareness about your body language, ask trusted co-workers and managers to give you feedback about your body language and how they interpret it. Given ways that others have described you in the past, take the time to notice your body language for the next week. What are your common gestures? Is it possible that these gestures are giving a message that is inconsistent with your intentions? If you become aware of an incongruent body gesture, then focus on changing it to reflect your true message and tone.

I once worked with a team where one of the supervisors used closed, disengaged body language. During the team-building session, as individuals were sharing their feelings about their workplace, he was slouched in his chair, looking down at the floor. At one point, I overheard a few staff members saying that he appeared disinterested. I took time with this supervisor and asked permission to share some feedback with him about how he was being experienced. He had never received feedback like this before. I coached him, giving suggestions about how to hold his body and telling him about the importance of eye contact. Then I asked him to sit in this new posture during the remainder of our team-building time. Staff members then remarked on how open and interested he appeared. They felt that he was truly listening to them.

Now that you've gained some insight into your body language, it would be helpful to ask yourself whether your non-verbal communication matches your words. When these two types of communication are congruent, people will naturally trust you more, and you will build rapport. Sometimes, when you're not confident about sharing a message, this disconnect may make you appear dishonest. People will know that something is amiss, but they may not take the time to understand you. They may find it easier simply to dismiss you.

When you understand these nuances of communication, both verbal and non-verbal, you can become a skilled communicator. Taking the time to reflect on interactions with others is a great way to understand how your message is being received. What did your listeners' body language tell you? Did they appear to be interested in what you were sharing? Did their faces show understanding or confusion? If they appeared confused, ask them what they understood about your message. Having your listeners repeat parts of your message will ensure that misunderstandings are avoided. And understanding your listeners' body language will give you immediate feedback.

Honest feedback given with the intention of helping another person is a true gift. However, it needs to be offered in a gentle, open manner and with permission. As a manager or supervisor, when you are clear about your communication strengths and challenges, you can give this gift to your staff members. Remember to check your words, your body language, and your gestures to ensure that you are consistent in sharing your message in a supportive manner that focuses on the growth of your staff members.

Remember Duke, whose message and body language were always congruent. Even though his feedback was negative, I heard him loud and clear!

~ 2 ~

Feedback:
Making Sure You're Heard

When we don't speak up and we allow others to treat us as they wish,
we give mixed messages about what is acceptable behaviour.

Duke spent a number of happy years with us until he passed away at a good, old age. Then, a little over two years ago, my husband and I decided to buy an adorable black Lab cross puppy—a black Lab crossed with another breed that we never did identify. Her name is Josee. She is vibrant, has high energy, and commonly challenges the rules set out for her. Her coat is almost entirely black and shiny, but she has a small, white marking on her chest and incredibly engaging dark brown eyes. Our good friends call her a whirling dervish, because she's so quick with everything she does.

Our neighbours Mitchell and Catherine have a Great Dane named Timothy, and Josee and this large dog are close friends. They spend a lot of time together, whether at our home, Mitchell's place, or our cottage. The two dogs have spent enough time together in all three locations that they know exactly where each other's toys are stored, and they just go in and help themselves to each other's stashes. Though they are so wrapped up in each other's lives, they have two different styles to get playtime going. Josee engages Timothy by coming head on and nudging him. Mr. Timothy is much more subtle in his approach: he often simply nods his head in Josee's direction. Because of this, it appears to the human element that Josee is always the instigator of high-energy play and that she is repeatedly picking on Timothy.

Josee and Timothy also have very different styles of engagement. Timothy plays hard for a few moments, then loses physical stamina and gets tired. Josee bounces around with energy that never stops. Despite their differences, they love to play and run together—they love just being together!

Josee also takes immense pleasure from teasing Timothy, and she does this by lying on his bed and holding one of his toys in her mouth. They engage in high-energy play—often tug or mock fighting. Their paws hit the floor, they growl at each other a lot, and because of Timothy's size, coupled with Josee's energy level, the whole process is quite overwhelming to the humans who are present. Josee can play for hours on end in this way. Because Timothy is a larger dog and of a breed that tends to have less energy and stamina, he often becomes exhausted by their interactions.

When Timothy tires out, he simply goes and lies down. Josee then runs over to him and keeps on playing. Though Timothy needs to sleep and truly wants to be left alone, he's too much the gentleman to tell her where to go. He just lifts a single paw and gently swipes at her. Josee takes this as a form of play and continues to engage until Timothy has fallen asleep. Even then, Josee will keep running up to him and sniff at his ears, trying to initiate more play. Since Timothy doesn't growl at her, as many dogs might, Josee, just like the Energizer Bunny, keeps on going and going.

Timothy's owner, Mitchell, and I have had several chats about Timothy's lack of setting boundaries with Josee. We wish he would learn to growl at her and tell her off so she'd get the message when enough is enough. Instead, it's always the humans who set the boundaries for Timothy. I think Josee secretly believes that if it wasn't for us people correcting her, Timothy would be just fine with her behaviour.

Do you experience times when a co-worker is engaging with you in a style that feels uncomfortable or overwhelming? As a manager or supervisor, do you set boundaries for your workers when they don't? Is there someone on your team who really needs to have more boundaries set and is not aware of it? What are your boundaries as a manager or supervisor?

When we don't speak up and we allow others to treat us as they wish, we give mixed messages about what is acceptable behaviour. If you continually tolerate something that is bothersome to you, one day you might explode and share your feelings about another person's behaviour in an aggressive manner. Your true message will then be lost, because the other person will hear your tone more than your message. That listener may then make an offhand remark about your mood and dismiss what you are telling them.

When we give each other honest feedback from a non-judgemental place, we can all grow together into our potential. Often, people find it difficult to offer direct and candid feedback, because they're afraid of what people might think of them or because they're concerned about the reaction they might get from another person. However, feedback, when appropriately delivered, is a true gift. It can help individuals gain a deeper understanding of their impact on other people, and it can help them grow as professionals.

Offering and receiving feedback can be extremely challenging. Over the years, I've witnessed several individuals who could become quite uncomfortable when receiving feedback, whether the comment was complimentary or critical. At performance appraisal time, for instance, managers and supervisors often have difficulty giving feedback about improvements that need to be made. But when you avoid giving this necessary feedback, you prevent your employee from making changes to help reach their full potential. All people need others to share with us what we are unable to see for ourselves.

So failing to give adequate feedback may result in a great employee not being aware of how much they are appreciated or, conversely, having a difficult employee remain unaware of the areas of growth for them. In most cases, feedback includes both praise and comments about areas of growth, and in this situation, the employee can benefit from each type of input.

As a manager or supervisor, it is important to lead the way in receiving and offering feedback. Do you ask for feedback on your ideas and performance? How do you hear feedback when it is given? Do you become defensive and shut down or do you listen openly and take the time to consider what you've heard and then reflect on how it may improve your work? It's a great idea to listen to the feedback and then give the individual a reflective statement about what you heard in *their* statement. This helps make communication clearer. It's also acceptable to ask the person to give you some time to think about what they've said before getting back to them.

It may be helpful to have a 360-degree review of your own performance. In this case, you would request either verbal or written feedback from those who work with you, those who report to you, your supervisors, your clients, and other stakeholders you interact with at your workplace. The results of this exercise will give you the opportunity to set clear goals for your ongoing growth as a leader.

We are all capable of becoming defensive, so if you need to offer feedback to an employee, colleague, or employer at any time, you can use techniques that will help that person hear your message fully, whether the feedback is positive or negative.

Here are some good questions to ask yourself prior to giving feedback:
- What is my motive?
- Am I coming from a place of frustration or a place of understanding?

- Am I giving feedback from a place of anger or from a place of mutual respect?
- Am I planning to criticize the other person or to share an honest insight?
- Do you have only your own best interests at heart or also those of the other person—or do you see both of you, ultimately, as the priority?
- What information do you need to share?
- What are the core issues at hand?

Make sure that you're coming from a place of compassion and understanding. Otherwise, you'll run the risk of being dismissed or ignored, as it can be very threatening to receive feedback. Once you're clear that your motive is to promote growth and understanding, it's time to prepare for giving feedback. First, reflect on what your message will be and then find a way to state it that shows understanding and does not put the other person in a corner. It may be helpful to jot down a few notes that you can refer to during your meeting with the other person. Once you know what you need to say and how you might share it with words that are non-judgemental, it's time to approach the other person. Make sure that you are specific in your feedback, stating clearly what your compliments and/or concerns are about.

To ensure that the person you are going to speak with is as open as possible, it may be important to set up an appointment time that works for both of you. This will ensure that the other person is not in the middle of a task that will take their attention away from your conversation.

The next step is to ask the other person whether you can give them some feedback. You might say, "Would you mind if I shared some thoughts with you?" Generally, people will say that they don't mind. As a manager or supervisor, you may need to give feedback even if the individual resists the idea. In this case, it may be helpful to say, "I have some concerns that

I need to share with you, and then we'll have time for you to ask any questions you need to ask." Then proceed with your concern.

I have found it beneficial in these circumstances to use the following template (ensuring you are using "I" statements):

When I experienced/heard/saw [describe the specific behaviour], my concern was [describe your concern in a non-judgemental manner].

For example, "When I saw your frequent trips to the coffee room, I became concerned that you might be distracting yourself from your work."

This type of statement is better than if you said something like "You go to the coffee machine so often that you're losing far too much time from your work." If you present your feedback as your own observation, rather than as a statement set in stone, you can give the other person the opportunity to present *their* view of the situation. This gives them an out. You may also want to ask if you've misunderstood them as you share your insights and experience.

The sandwich method is also effective. According to this approach, you always start with a positive statement (perhaps something you appreciate about working with this person or a skill they have that you admire). Share the concern and then offer another positive comment.

Once, when I was at a placement to get experience in social work, I was given some very challenging, negative feedback. As I was feeling insecure in those days, I agreed with the individual who was giving the feedback. I basically agreed that I did not have the skills to be a social worker and that I would make a better medical secretary. I was devastated and went to my placement coordinator, Susan, who gave me some very sage advice—when receiving negative feedback, never agree immediately. Ask for some time to think about it and get back to the person. As a very young woman, had I done this, I would not have felt so humiliated and embarrassed. By giving yourself time to process the information, you can return to the situation with a clear head and take responsibility for yourself in a proactive manner.

Here's an old adage about responding to negative feedback: If you hear something once from one individual, it is their opinion and may or may not be relevant to you. If you hear the same or similar feedback from more than one source, it is time to step back, look at the comments, and identify what you're doing that is creating that opinion in others.

When you offer vague feedback, people may feel confused or set up for failure. I have personally been given feedback from a supervisor beginning with "Other people experience you as," with no specific examples and no names. It was impossible for me to work with this feedback. In fact, I began to become a little suspicious of others, wondering which of my co-workers had gone to my supervisor without coming to me first. As a result, I did not grow from this feedback.

As a supervisor or manager, ensure that your feedback is coming from a place of understanding, for the purpose of growth. Take the time to prepare. Make your statements both respectful and clear. Ask the individual what they heard you say, to ensure that your message is understood.

~ 3 ~

Curiosity

When encountering new people and concepts,
let your curiosity overcome fear of change.

I was sitting beside my friend Mitchell at a Christmastime house party. The living room was cozy, a toasty fire was burning in the fireplace, and we were sipping on wine from elegant glasses. But Mitchell was feeling badly that his Great Dane, Timothy (first introduced in Chapter 2), was spending such long hours in his crate every day. Mitchell and his wife had hectic work schedules, and they just didn't have as much time as they wanted, to spend with their pet. As we chatted about the differences in our schedules, mine virtually empty at the time, he asked if I might think about becoming Timothy's dog walker. I said yes and felt honoured that they trusted me with their precious Mr. Timothy. The Great Dane and I began our twice-weekly walks a few days later.

As a Great Dane, Mr. Timothy is not a lightweight. He tips the scales at 125 pounds and could easily crush any small object he might sit on. But he's a gentle, slow-moving pooch, and we quickly fell into our walking routine. He would tend to wander behind me, sniffing and doing his doggy business—obviously very happy to be outside. He'd taught me that should he react, I needed to be very quick to correct him—as soon as I felt any slight jerk on the leash. Otherwise, I'd be looking up as he'd be looking down on me, wondering what I was doing lying on the ground.

By May, on the day we met Lily, we were well into a routine and had developed our own communication during walks. We were completely comfortable with each other. This particular spring afternoon, we'd set out for our regular constitutional shortly after lunch. We were heading down the sidewalk in an affluent residential area, with large houses on each side of the road, many with spacious porches furnished with wicker settees and chairs. The lawns were nicely manicured, and the flower gardens had been tended with loving care. I could picture Victorian ladies sipping tea on those porches on a hot summer day.

As we rounded the corner, I heard a kind, soft voice calling, "Come here, Lily. Here Lily." As I looked to see what kind of dog this Lily might be, I was surprised to see a pot-bellied pig returning to her owner. As a farmer's daughter, I had to giggle, watching a pig actually coming when called—something I'd never seen before. Lily was small—perhaps six inches tall—and as cute as a button, with a small black patch around her left eye.

As we continued to walk, we came closer to the little animal, and Timothy noticed her, examining her with great curiosity. Then Lily saw Timothy, and she ran as fast as her little legs could take her *towards* the huge dog. As if they were in the movies, their eyes locked, they were magnetically drawn together, and time seemed to slow down. Lily came right up to Timothy, and he responded by dropping his head to sniff the pig. They were exploring each other nose to nose—even though Timothy's head was almost as big as Lily's entire body! They sniffed each other for a few minutes—obviously completely enamoured with each other. It was as if Timothy had found the most interesting creature of his lifetime, and Lily was reflecting back his love.

All of a sudden, Timothy flinched, and I immediately became concerned about Lily's future. So I snapped back to reality and said,

"Leave it," to make sure Timothy didn't hurt the little pig by mistake. Timothy obeyed me, walking towards me and following my lead as I took him away from the scene. But he turned his head around 180 degrees so he could keep gazing at Lily. And though Lily's owner was calling her, the little pig ran after us. I felt as if I'd just broken up the biggest love affair of all time. Timothy kept staring back at Lily until we turned the corner and he could no longer see her.

Later, I thought about how these two species were willing to explore each other fearlessly despite their obvious differences. The encounter was a brand-new experience for both of them, but their curiosity helped them overcome their differences and any fear they might have had about each other. I began to consider how curiosity can be beneficial in the team environment. Just like Timothy and Lily, teams can use curiosity as a technique to discover and understand new concepts and ideas.

What does your team do when introduced to a new concept? Do they seek first to understand or do they close down? How do you react even to the word "change" when it is used? Are you excited by the opportunities or do you feel a sense of internal resistance? Some people will shut down and immediately reject the change before even considering it. This is not too surprising, since change is commonly viewed with fear. Team members may worry about what might happen if they don't embrace a change, or they may be concerned that they don't have the skills needed for a new project.

Creating an open dialogue will help your team members come on board and embrace changes. Get to know which team members become most fearful and help them through the change by reminding them about the supports, courses, or training they will receive. Help them recognize that by putting fear aside and replacing it with curiosity, they will benefit greatly.

Individuals can suffer from change fatigue, a condition that happens when change is so constant that it becomes exhausting. A great deal of energy is needed to cope with the increasing demands that result from adjusting to new concepts and ideas. So individuals and teams alike can shut down and create resistance, unknowingly sabotaging the proposed innovations. This can cause stagnation in the team, a sense of being blocked, which, in turn, slows down or stops the flow of new ideas and creativity. When this happens to your team, it is helpful to stop and take stock of where your team is at. It may be a great time to bring in some employee recognition to let them know their efforts are appreciated. This is covered later in Chapter 13.

As a team member, if you can be like Timothy and Lily by using curiosity when new information, ideas, and concepts arise, you will be able to alleviate a great deal of stress for yourself, your team, and even your supervisor or manager. By being open and inquisitive, you will also see possibilities and options that you may not have thought of before. If Timothy had simply ignored Lily and walked past her, he would not have expanded his horizons or his knowledge base. But because he remained open and curious and explored the strange being, he fell in love with the new. How might you benefit from an upcoming change?

When a new change is about to be implemented, as a manager or supervisor, it may be advantageous to hold a question period where your staff members are able to ask questions and get direct, honest answers about the change. Set up clear parameters for the meeting. Let your staff know what is written in stone and what elements of the upcoming change are open for discussion. For example, the innovation may be a directive from upper management, yet the method the team uses to implement the change may be open to discussion. Let staff know how much time will be allotted for questions. Present clear boundaries for the meeting, and let your staff know when you are looking for input and when you want to just describe the upcoming change. This approach will help your staff feel respected and will also help them figure out where to direct their energy.

At one workplace, management asked their employees for input about a change that was coming up. The team misunderstood and thought that their ideas would affect the way the new program was going to be implemented. They excitedly gave their input—only to find out later that management had already decided who would be involved in the implementation and how it would be handled. The team members felt frustrated and disrespected, because it seemed to them that their opinions were not valued. Had the managers communicated clearly that management had already made the decision and that they were simply notifying the team members of an upcoming change, the staff would have responded in a different manner: asking questions, rather than offering suggestions about the change.

As long as you clarify what input is welcomed, open question-and-answer periods will bring great benefits—simply by demonstrating that you respect your employees' need to understand the new initiative. You may also encounter a positive side effect. If team members question a change, they may identify a possible difficulty, and that will allow you to come up with a remedy before the problem actually arises.

As a manager or supervisor, you will improve the process by asking relevant, open-ended questions to help your staff investigate new options.

- What is interesting about this initiative?
- What part of this concept is most intriguing to you?
- If the idea were adopted, how might it help you do your job?
- What part of the implementation process would you like to be involved in?
- How might you grow as a professional by being involved in this initiative?
- What skills might you acquire during this change?

Through positive inquiry, you may instill curiosity in your staff. They might just find that the idea they thought was not worth exploring is the very one they want to experience "nose to nose", and they may then fall in love with the change.

When an environment of curiosity is created, your team members will be more open minded, and they will therefore tend to be more creative and innovative. The underlying values in the team will become trust, cooperation, and acceptance. This underpinning will allow your employees to feel valued and appreciated for their input and ideas, and individuals will therefore be able to share their ideas more easily. Although they will know that their suggestions may not be adopted in their entirety, they'll be aware that their concepts will be viewed as having merit. An idea may become just one of the building blocks for completing the project or for working together in a collaborative way, but it will be valued as part of the overall scheme. In this way, individuals in the team will become excited about sharing their ideas and posing questions, since they'll trust that all team members are being supportive and curious.

As your employees are discussing the upcoming change, it will be helpful to talk about all aspects of the idea: the good, the not-so-good, and even the ugly. When team members comment on all elements of the innovation with curiosity and respect, they can play an active role in creating the most positive approach. The team's analysis will be most successful if team members first listen to the idea and then explore it by asking the following essential questions:

- How much can we gain from this idea?
- What might hold us back from moving to the best solution?
- How, collectively, should we address the parts that simply need to be changed or revamped, in order to take this idea from good to great?

As questions are asked and all team members answer them, they can take a not-so-good idea and alter it until it becomes a breakthrough approach.

How a team decides what to keep, what to discard, and what to simply alter is of vital importance. Taking the time to listen openly to one another and ensuring that ego does not lead the discussion will help you move the process forward. Before you start the discussion, it can be a help to specify a timeframe, set a consistent tone of cooperation, and nurture a spirit of creativity. Also remember to make your staff aware of the parameters for input: what is open for discussion and what has already been decided by management.

As a manager or supervisor, when bringing potential changes to the team, be careful to remain open to feedback and to view it through the lens of your ultimate goal: continuous improvement. When you remain open, the team will know you value their input, and then they'll be more likely to discuss their reservations up front. This creates an atmosphere of trust and openness, which will be more likely to result in the support of all team members. Some people need to question a new concept or idea before they can adopt it. Only when they've had the opportunity to state their concerns and objectives directly can they move forward on an idea. Back on the street with Lily, the pot-bellied pig, I allowed Timothy to explore and use his curiosity, but after a while, I also had to put an end to it. In the same way, at some point, you will need to shift your team from questioning to accepting and then moving on to action on a new project.

However, be sure not to cut off discussion too soon. When team members are given enough time to express themselves, they will know that they are trusted and understood, and this relieves stress for everyone. We all want to work in an environment where change is less challenging and easier to adopt.

So the next time you approach a new idea or concept in your workplace, create an atmosphere where your employees can be like Timothy and Lily, setting aside any fear and exploring the new with curiosity and openness. You'll be amazed at the results.

~ 4 ~

Positive Focus: The "Dreaded Three"

*With dogs and teams, the best results come from
focusing on positive outcomes.*

One day, Josee and I were headed downtown to my bank, where I was going to pay a bill. At a pleasant pace, that walk takes about 15 minutes from our front door. Some of the sidewalks still had snow on them, but others had been graciously cleared by the owners. The temperature was comfortable—slightly above freezing—so our walk was relaxed despite the slightly overcast skies.

Dog walking is a meditative experience for me, a time of personal reflection, and on this particular afternoon, I was busy reviewing my day and some challenging conversations I had experienced. I went into automatic mode, not really paying much attention to Josee. As I mentioned in Chapter 2, Josee is an exuberant dog. In fact, she's so energetic that many people mistake her for a young puppy despite her actual age of two years, five months. She is also inquisitive and interested in everything that is happening around her.

Josee was excitedly sniffing something just beyond the end of her leash, or perhaps she was contemplating jumping up to say hello and give kisses to a passerby. Whatever she was doing, it pulled me out of my self-reflective state. Though Josee loves jumping up on people, I find this habit obnoxious and am actively teaching her not to do this—but it's a work in progress. There is a certain interested look that strangers give Josee—the one where they look at her as if to say, "You are so cute." This makes my bouncy black Lab cross think she has licence to fully engage with them. When this happens, I pull down on her leash to restrain her and verbally correct her. But as I listened to myself that day, I noticed I was coming out with a barrage of the word "no."

What message was I really sending to Josee? I wondered. An important dog-training concept is that canines learn through repetition and through hearing the same, clear command, given with the expectation of consistent behaviour. This approach creates the best-trained mutts. I realized that I needed to get back to basics with training Josee and to use the command "off" when she tried to jump up. Only then would she be clear about what I expected.

When we were in obedience class with Josee, the trainers told us to reserve the word "no" for emergency situations, where safety was an issue. This way, she would be clear about what we were expecting her to do, and our commands would be more likely to succeed.

In fact, I was saying "no" to Josee so frequently on this walk that I clicked into my personal commitment to eliminate that word from my vocabulary—a commitment that I'd made only the day before. That day, I'd participated in a teleseminar with Michael Losier, the law of attraction expert. The seminar was hosted by my professional association, the Canadian Association of Professional Speakers (CAPS). CAPS makes these sessions available throughout the year as continuing education for its members. The seminars are each one hour long, which makes it easy to listen in and then get back to work. I was excited to listen to this particular presentation, hoping that I would pick up a few hints about how to improve my manifesting skills. (Manifesting is the skill of attracting what you want in your life through intention and positive focus.) Michael spoke about his success in business, which he has experienced as a result of using his techniques. He also described how he has used the power of positive thinking to help him in making life decisions.

One of the great tips that Michael shared in that seminar was to remove three words from our vocabulary—specifically, "no," "not," and "don't." He noted that we manifest what we focus on. When we tell ourselves or someone else what we do "not" desire, we are actually focusing on, or giving energy to, the undesired situation. It is much more effective to focus on what we really want in our lives. So I decided to work on the elimination process and began with awareness, which is always the first step in creating change. I had actually heard this information before Michael's seminar, and although it is not new to me, I still need reminders to keep myself on track. I was surprised by the number of times I was using these "dreaded three" words in my life.

As a co-worker or supervisor, do you notice how many times you use the "dreaded three" in a day? Are you perceived as a naysayer or someone who is disagreeable? Where is your focus? Is it on what can go wrong or what solutions can be found? Are you a cautious person who fears change and innovation?

How many times are you driving to work, running a bit late, and thinking, I "don't" want a red light—only to hit one red light after the other? Michael would change it up and say, "Thank you for all the green lights." Give it a try and see what happens.

When we focus on the "no," "not," "don't" pattern of thinking, we create a negative situation in our minds, our team, and our environment. Think of a time when someone started a conversation with you, using the word "no" or "don't." I'll bet you started to feel a bit disheartened, thinking you were "not" likely going to get your desired outcome. Or perhaps you felt as if you were being corrected in a negative way.

I have noticed that people do actually have particular reactions to the word "no." Think about a visit to the grocery store. We have all witnessed situations where a young child asked for a treat and the parent said, "No." The result is almost always an unhappy, crying child. Saying "no" in the workplace creates the risk of shutting down an inspired process that may have resulted in exceeding the team's goal.

As a manager or supervisor, it's vital to use clear, positive language to ask for what you desire from your team members. This creates an open environment, where individuals begin to consider the value of your goal. It tends to engage others in the team, creating more team cohesion. When clarity is achieved, all members of the team can offer input and begin to work on the task at hand. Your staff will know what you want, and they won't need to waste time trying to figure that out.

This positive and concise form of communication can result in collaboration and cooperation. But how do you shift from a "no," "not," and "don't" form of communication to constructive and upbeat messages?

First, start by just listening to yourself and noticing how many times during a day, a meeting, or an interaction you use the "dreaded three" words. Ask yourself, "What is causing this focus on the 'no' word?" If you find that you are overusing these words, start to think about how you could change your dialogue to focus on positive, desired outcomes, rather than the obstacles. Ask yourself what you want instead of the potential problems that are taking centre stage. Do your words actually reflect your goals?

Keep working on changing your focus until the outcome you need becomes crystal clear in your mind. This step will prepare you to communicate your request to the team in a more easily understandable way. And your positive presentation of the issues may even allow your team to explode into great success.

Here are some questions you can ask yourself, to clarify your goals:

- Am I clear about what is needed? If not, what information do I need to find in order to get more clarity? Through which people or sources will I be able to find this information?

- How can I share my message with the team in a positive, clear, and concise manner?
- How can I word my request, using only positive phrasing?
- Have I made my expectations and goals clear to the team?
- Did I use any of the "dreaded three" in the wording of my request? If so, how can I rephrase my statement in a positive way?

If you are using the "dreaded three" during interactions, how can you switch the word "no" to a question that would evoke curiosity instead? For example, "How might we explore other solutions to our current pricing challenge?" A question like this is called an "open-ended question," because it can't be answered with a "yes" or a "no." It invites dialogue. Conversely, a close-ended question results in a "yes" or "no" response. For example, consider the following two questions:

- Did you think about the logistics of this program? (closed-ended question)
- What aspects of the logistics have you considered in your plan? (open-ended question)

The first question above is a close-ended question, and it has an undertone of judgement, while the second question invites an open dialogue and provides more information for the listener to respond to. By asking open-ended questions, you can initiate productive conversations about the project at hand.

Positive words and clear, positive goals also encourage productive dialogue when different team members do not agree with each other. If one team member has a difference with another, the "dreaded three" will only increase the tension between the two. However, if you create a culture in which people are encouraged to always look at the goal of the group in positive ways, and if team members are coached to present concerns about differences in a respectful manner, everyone will have a greater sense of security within the team. By knowing that others will work on building them up as opposed to criticizing them and shooting their efforts down, all your employees will function at a higher level and will create and execute more successful, well-thought-out plans.

The "yes anding" technique is a great one for creating more positive conversations. It originated in improv theatre, where actors have no script but improvise, instead, right on stage. For an improv scene to be successful, each actor must build on the lines the other actor or actors say (or on gestures given). These are called the "offer" and the "response." First, one actor provides an offer (a beginning statement or gesture). Then the second actor adds to that offer by creating a response that builds on the first actor's statement or gesture.

This "yes anding" theatrical technique can also be extremely effective in supporting fellow team members. Imagine that someone is working on a project and considering its logistics. As you listen, you realize that they haven't considered another project that will impact the timing. You have options in presenting your thoughts. You could say, "What about the dates of Project X?" or you could use the "yes anding" technique and say, "Yes, your timeline sounds reasonable, and I am wondering how your timeline will be impacted by Project X?" Notice how the "yes and" format invites more dialogue and sounds less like a judgement.

On the improv stage, "yes anding" helps create hilarious skits based on cooperation and actors adding to each other's ideas. You can also use this technique to facilitate brainstorming techniques in the office. As people offer their thoughts, simply have them start their sentences with "yes and." In this way, their ideas won't be blocked, and every notion will be accepted. The point of a brainstorming session is not to judge but to generate ideas, and the sky's the limit when your team brainstorms using this technique.

On one occasion, when I was preparing to facilitate a team dynamics workshop, I used the "yes anding" technique. This helped a manager accept my interviewing staff before our team session. When I first made this request, he'd said no. He was concerned that staff members would only complain, as opposed to providing constructive input. I responded to his initial reaction by saying that I understood his concerns ("yes"), and I went on to say that I found the interviewing process helpful, since it always allowed me to gain awareness of the staff's perspective. This, in turn, would create a more beneficial workshop. The manager agreed to my speaking directly with his staff, and this resulted in a powerful experience. Because I got to know each individual before the workshop, team dynamics were addressed more directly, and there was significant positive change in the team's level of functioning.

When you shift your inner focus to the positive and this is reflected in your interactions with your team, you will influence your team in a positive manner. Research has shown that when individuals are positively focused, they are more likely to engage in constructive processes and be more creative in their work. This, combined with open-ended questions and the "yes and" technique, will encourage your team to have more open discussions about projects. The ultimate outcome will be better-constructed plans of action, resulting in more success.

The spirit of collaboration and cooperation that is created by these three simple techniques—focusing on the desired outcome, asking open-ended questions, and "yes anding"—helps all team members know that they will be supported in their attempts to work with the team. Imagine having all team members "yes anding" each other's ideas. Then the power of positive thinking will be at work, creating amazing results!

Help your team members function like Josee, who responds best when I focus on giving her clear, positive directions and when I "yes and" her attempts at positive behaviour.

~ 5 ~

Conflict

*Conflict is a natural phenomenon
that is best dealt with and then released.*

Exhibition Park, a mere two blocks from our home, is one of Josee's favourite playgrounds. Outlined by four streets, the park is filled with mature maple trees that form a canopy of shade in the summer and display vibrant colours in the fall. There's a baseball diamond at one end and a football field at the other, with a large, grassy area in between. Depending on the time of day, Josee may be the only dog in the park or there could be up to 35 canines clustered or running in various groups.

One chilly fall morning, wrapped up in a warm sweater, I took Josee to the park. Our usual route winds along a gravel hiking trail situated between two rows of homes. Though it's in the middle of the city, it's a peaceful place, and that morning, the trees lining our path were just beginning to turn colour. It was early enough that the dew was still on the grass.

But the peace was broken shortly after we entered the park and walked up to the baseball diamond. There, the only other dog in the park—Comet, a large Border Collie cross—was playing with a stick. Tracey, Comet's owner, would throw the stick, Comet would retrieve it, and they carried on with this game for several minutes. Before long, Josee was running around, chasing Comet. Then Josee decided she wanted to play with the stick, so she grabbed it and ran off. Not surprisingly, Comet was not pleased and wanted the stick back. Before Tracey and I knew it, our two dogs were growling, with their hair raised up on the backs of their necks, and then they launched into a fight. We were both shocked! By the time we realized they were having a set-to, it was over. The entire skirmish had lasted no more than 30 seconds.

After the fight, Comet placed his head over Josee's head. In dog language, this meant that Comet was telling Josee that he was the alpha dog—the top dog, who gets fed first and gets the toys first. Only when he's finished eating or playing can the other dogs in the pack help themselves or have fun with the toys. Josee accepted his message, so now they were both clear on each other's roles. They'd come to an agreement as to who was in charge and what the expectations were. Josee then let Comet have the stick and didn't touch it again.

Tracey and I stood with confused looks on our faces, wondering why all of a sudden, at the ripe old age of one year, these dogs would have a fight. Next thing we knew, our pets were playing as if nothing had happened. It was as if Josee and Comet had completely let go of the issue. They began to wrestle together with friendly body language and amicable noises. They were having a ball together.

It struck me at that moment that if humans could learn this lesson of having a disagreement, dealing directly with it, and not taking it personally (as Josee and Comet did), we would be much happier and much less stressed. Canine behaviour can also provide a great example of how to effectively deal with conflict, in order to minimize the impact on the team. When team members do not deal with differences well, their animosity tends to fester away and then becomes a sore spot in the dynamics of the entire team.

People typically deal with conflict in one of three ways:

1. Some require time to process the facts and to analyze the situation before talking about it.

2. Others need to deal with the conflict right away and will promptly seek others out to work things through.

3. Others fear conflict and do their best to avoid it.

When two of these three conflict-management styles interact, misunderstandings and a high level of stress can be the result. People who prefer conflict-management style 2 may believe that others are simply avoiding the issue. Conversely, individuals who require time or want to avoid conflict can feel rushed by those who want to deal with the conflict as soon as possible.

People who cope with conflict by avoidance or aggression are expensive to the team's function. When individuals are indirect in their conflict-management style, they tend to become stressed; they tend to gossip and try to get others on their side. Suddenly, the team will be divided, and the leader (and the team members) won't even know why.

When a person uses aggression to stifle conflict, other team members tend to feel bullied and may shut down and stop interacting with that person. They may need support, so they may talk to other team members about the conflict, sometimes creating divided loyalties. Again, the dynamics of gossiping will appear and the team will be divided.

I have worked on teams where unresolved conflicts were so intense that individuals ended up going on stress leave. They felt no support from the team and even felt attacked by team members. Some of this conflict was a result of management failing to identify role responsibilities clearly. But once a meeting was held to clarify the role confusion, team work became more cooperative.

When conflict arises on a team, it means that team members have different points of view or that a misunderstanding has occurred. Then, if two team members, for instance, have different conflict-management styles, each of them may assume that the other person is being difficult or is trying to be manipulative. When we personalize conflict, we may fall into believing that the other individual is intending harm. But most often, in workplace discord, no harm is intended. When we realize that the person we are quarrelling with is simply holding onto their opinion and not intending to hurt us, it can be easier to let go of the anger and move towards resolution.

Sitting down together to openly share individual perspectives creates an opportunity for understanding and respect. And situations become clearer when people disclose their personal points of view, including the values that motivated their behaviour. When the two parties are unable to resolve the conflict on their own, they may require an impartial observer, such as a supervisor or manager. If you are that supervisor or manager, it will be important for you to listen to both people, being careful not to take sides, and to ensure that each individual is heard by the other. It is helpful to ask each person to listen, with an open mind, without interrupting, while the second party is sharing and vice versa. You may wish to tell each team member that they are both partly right. This will help reassure them that you are not judging or taking sides.

You may need to assist people who are avoiders to understand the value in having a respectful conversation. Your presence alone may help them be more comfortable with the process. And prior to the meeting, you should ask each individual some helpful questions, such as the following:

- What, according to your understanding, was the other party attempting to share, do, or say?
- What were your key points?
- What, according to your understanding, did the other individual say in response to your key points? (This way, you may remember an important response that you've previously missed.)

- Was this what you were attempting to communicate?
- What might make it easier to listen to the other person in the future?
- Do you understand how this misunderstanding occurred?
- Is there anything that you might need to take responsibility for in relation to the other person?
- What do you need to do to resolve this conflict more fully?
- What are you willing to let go?
- Do you want to be right or do you want to be happy?
- What might you have done differently now that we have explored this?
- Where do we need to go from here to ensure that you and your teammate have a positive working relationship?

Ask each person to share their perspective on what happened, using "I" statements. For example, if Comet were to have spoken to Josee about the stick incident, he might have said, "When I watched you take the stick, I was afraid that I would lose it, because in the past, other dogs have never brought my stick back."

These interchanges are most successful when the speaker describes behaviour and doesn't make judgements that sound accusatory. Ask each speaker to be clear and concise. This will often help the listener become less defensive.

The basic formula is this: "When I observed/experienced [behaviour], I felt [emotion] because [thought or reason you felt that way].

During the resolution meeting, have each individual state what they heard the other person say. If one person did not believe the other party understood them correctly, give that person an opportunity to clarify what they said. In this way, you'll ensure that each person feels they have been heard. By deeply listening and hearing one another, mutual understanding and respect can be developed.

Once this mutual respect has been created, it gives room for stronger team interaction. Individuals will begin to listen more completely to one another, reflecting back what they heard, to ensure that they absolutely understood the other person's point of view. There may be times when team members experience a difference of opinion that results in gridlock. In cases like these, use the "agree-to-disagree principle": I respect your right to your opinion, and you respect my right to my thoughts too. We agree to put team needs first despite these differing perspectives.

One of the essential behaviours required for such an exchange is the willingness to listen fully to the other person. For a few moments, each individual needs to be prepared to suspend their opinion in order to create an openness to explore the other person's position. Then each person needs to be willing to recognize the validity of the other person's viewpoint, share their understanding of what the other person said, and then, based on mutual respect, proceed to create the options that are available for this particular issue.

If one individual refuses to engage in this resolution process, you, as supervisor or manager, will need to pull that person aside and help them work through the process described above before having a three-way meeting. If the person has an attitude problem, you'll need to share your observations about this and offer the individual feedback about how you have witnessed this behaviour impacting the team. Conversely, if the person has felt the other party has been bullying them, you will need to deal with that directly. Bullying will be covered in Chapter 20.

We all arrive at our perspectives based on our own experiences and the way that we perceive the world. Sometimes, we make assumptions that are not based on reality. So we need to check out our points of view, to make sure that our assumptions are accurate in a given situation. And when we have made an incorrect guess, as Josee did when she took Comet's stick, we need to promptly acknowledge that, take responsibility for what we've said or done, and, like Josee and Comet, be willing to let go of the disagreement.

As a team member, it's vital to fully suspend your judgement, listen to every team member's input in its entirety (even when you have a differing point of view), and respect the fact that their idea has some merit. When you do this, you'll be helping to create an incredible workplace, where differences of opinion can be resolved easily. When all members of the team adopt the core value of respect, the team becomes a place where individuals are motivated, creative, and can't wait to get to work in the morning.

Resolving conflict in teams is paramount to reducing stress and creating a positive working environment. As a supervisor or manager, it is your role to help individuals go through the conflict-resolution process if they are unable to do so themselves. Once conflict is resolved, productivity will naturally soar within the team environment. Individuals can work all out on a project together and can even play hard together in the process.

Imagine the fun Josee and Comet would have missed if they had continued to fight over the stick. By airing their conflict in a direct manner, they quickly found a resolution and got back to the business of playing with each other.

~ 6 ~

Self-Confidence versus Ego

*In the canine world, having a realistic understanding
of strengths and weaknesses creates self-confidence in action.*

Josee has always been a confident being. When we were considering adopting her, I went to observe her behaviour and discovered a self-assured little five-month-old puppy. Though there were plenty of fancy toys lying around on the floor in her area, she chose a stick from outside and sat down to chew on it. As she chomped on her delightful find, her eyes showed pure pleasure. She knew who she was and was okay with it. She didn't need high-end toys to play with. She was self-sufficient.

At the park, when we throw the Frisbee to Josee, she jumps to catch it and is sure that she'll get it. She leaps into the air like a skilled Olympic high jumper, ready to catch—and her confidence shows on her face as well. Whenever she misses, she simply runs over to the Frisbee and picks it up. She doesn't get upset or critical, because the thrill of the chase is just as important as the big catch. She knows that success and failure are both part of the game. And she gets equal pleasure from catching the Frisbee whether or not she's being watched.

Josee is willing to take on new risks and even fail. Instead of hanging her head in embarrassment if she fumbles, she has a so-what's-next attitude. At times, she's at risk of being too full of herself and having too much ego. So we make sure to teach her that while she's important, we are the leaders of our pack. We do simple things like having her wait until Mark and I enter the house before she comes in and having her sit and wait for her food until she's given permission to eat. While these measures may seem to demonstrate arrogance on our part, given Josee's personality, they are much needed to help her understand her place in the world. This way, she remains a balanced dog. It is our responsibility to ensure that she is treated in a manner that she will understand and to bring out her best traits and reduce her weaknesses.

Humans tend not to be as self-assured and are therefore sometimes driven by ego. Although an overinflated ego may appear to be the same as self-confidence, it's actually often a reflection of a poor self-image. When a person's ego needs to be petted, or reinforced, the individual will appear to be overly dependent on getting praise and validation. So they become upset when they are not receiving positive strokes. When ego is the central pillar of their lives, they will do whatever they can to get attention. When they are not receiving the attention they crave, they feel inadequate. Their competitive drive to be best and to surpass everyone else then becomes so strong that they'll do whatever they can to prove they're the most important. The person propelled by ego needs will put themselves first and ignore the needs of others. In other words, they could be described as arrogant.

Self-confident individuals, on the other hand, know their abilities and have a healthy ego. They do not require praise to be motivated and to feel okay. In fact, the confident worker will know the areas in which they are highly skilled, but they will also have sufficient inner strength to tell the team and supervisor about areas where they need help. They are willing to take on new challenges and realize that they can learn new behaviours and skills.

The difference between self-confidence and egotistical behaviour can be huge in humans. When a person is suffering from arrogance, they will brag about their abilities. They may take on a task, saying it's a breeze, even though they don't know how to do it. They are less likely to ask for help when they're stuck. After all, they don't want anyone to know their weaknesses. They're apt to make excuses about why they couldn't complete the task at hand instead of admitting that they failed. They tend to become negative when they struggle and will come up with excuses for their failure: something else was faulty; someone else didn't do their part. When they do a job well, they expect praise and may become resentful if they don't get the public recognition they feel they deserve.

The arrogant worker may also take credit for another's work, since their inner need for validation to feel okay may override their sense of right and wrong. For them, the inner fear of inadequacy will prevent them from being honest and acknowledging others for a job well done. They may communicate the attitude "Well, any dummy could do that."

One time, a team member, Dionne, came to another team member, Samantha, in a panic, asking for help in dealing with a client who was in crisis because of an addiction issue. Samantha coached her so she could understand the specific steps she needed to take and even made calls to help her get the client to a treatment centre that afternoon. The plan required a lot of creativity because resources were limited. But once the plans were put in place, Dionne relaxed.

Afterwards, during a team meeting, their manager mentioned what an incredible job Dionne had done in getting the client to treatment. Dionne sat and soaked up the positive feedback and never mentioned Samantha's role in the situation. Her lack of confidence caused her to hide behind her co-worker's knowledge and to take the credit for Samantha's planning. As a result of her behaviour, Samantha felt taken for granted. And the next time Dionne bragged about what she'd accomplished, Samantha wondered whether she had truly done the work herself or whether she was taking credit for someone else's work again.

41

People who are self-confident are willing to acknowledge both their talents and their challenges. They will seek help when needed, knowing that this will improve their skill levels. They are realistic about their capabilities. When they take on new challenges, they will ask questions in order to ascertain what the expectations are and where they can receive assistance when needed. They will quietly complete tasks for the internal reward of a job well done.

As a manager or supervisor, it is important to be self-confident and not ego driven. Check yourself against the characteristics described in the last paragraph. Have you received any feedback during your life suggesting that you've been aloof or arrogant? What is your body language saying?

Think of others whom you have experienced as egotistical and write down any behaviours that you felt communicated their sense of self-importance.

- How did they stand?
- How did they speak to others?
- What was their tone of voice?
- What did their facial expression reveal?
- How did they deal with feedback—whether negative or positive?

Now ask yourself whether any of these characteristics could describe you. If you have difficulty doing this self-assessment, you could ask someone you trust who would give you honest feedback from a place of gentle kindness.

If you think you're suffering from egotistical behaviour, take a deep breath. You are not alone. Many of us have some area in our lives where we act or have acted egotistically. Reflect on what your skills really are. Don't embellish them. Be straight with yourself. What are your standards for yourself? Are they the same as for other people? If they differ, ask yourself these questions: In what ways? What motivates me to act in this manner? How do I view myself differently from others? Is this a fair assessment?

Now you need to look at what you are willing to change in this area. Since personal change is often difficult, we need and deserve support when embarking on such a mission. So it would be a good idea to enlist the help of a therapist or coach to help you move away from areas where you have a tendency to egotistical behaviour—intentional or not.

When dealing with your team, it's important to give them a sense of some of your weaknesses, as well as your strengths. Don't pretend that you're highly skilled in all areas. A well-rounded supervisor or manager is able to make an honest appraisal of their characteristics—the ones that enhance skill and personality and the ones that detract from them. As you role-model confident behaviour and allow your staff to assist you in your areas of challenge, your workers will know that they too can be human, that they're not expected to be perfect. Like you, they don't need to hide their areas of growth and can turn them into learning goals.

As a manager or supervisor, if you have a team member who shows arrogance (bragging endlessly about accomplishments, dismissing other people's input or value), meet with them privately and help them do a realistic appraisal of their strengths. Here's a four-step process to follow:

1. Ask them what they are really good at. Have them give evidence of this. The purpose of this question is not to challenge them but to help them acquire a more accurate perception of themselves.

2. Next, have your team member outline areas where they need to grow. You might ask, "In what areas do you think you'd benefit from learning more?" By wording this question in a positive way, you will be less likely to trigger the vulnerability that caused the arrogant behaviour in the beginning.

3. Ask your team member what they would like to work on and help them set realistic goals—goals that are measurable,

attainable, and time specific. Then help them break these goals into smaller, more manageable steps. This will help them see their progress and be motivated to continue towards the desired outcome.

4.   Help your team member when there's a setback in learning new behaviours. Review what they did well, rather than saying that they failed, and point out where they showed progress and how they could improve the next time around. Remind your team member that any growth they make is a step towards developing more real self-confidence.

If you find that an arrogant person on your staff is taking credit for the work of others, take them aside and ask questions about the process they went through to complete the task. Ask who helped them with the project. Suggest that they go back to the team and own up to their behaviour. This allows the individual to save face, rather than being embarrassed by being drawn out during a team meeting. Remember that arrogance is a function of lack of self-esteem. So it will be important to make sure that you give an arrogant team member credit where it is due without overpraising them. Help them see that acknowledging their humanness will be a huge benefit as they go on their way through life. As humans, we are never perfect, and expecting anything close to perfection from yourself or another person is simply unrealistic. Unrealistic expectations have been called "premeditated disappointments." Don't set yourself or another person up for this kind of outcome.

On the other hand, you may have a staff member who is very confident and completes tasks well but doesn't fully acknowledge the skills and strengths they have. Give this person recognition as a way of honouring their true abilities and as a method of helping them take ownership of those skills and other abilities they have. (For more about this subject, see Chapter 13, Treats and Employee Appreciation.)

A good supervisor or manager encourages all team members to accept themselves fully—with their strengths and their areas of growth. It's a good idea to take some proactive measures that will help your staff explore what changes they might like to make in their behaviours. This will help them develop as people and also contribute greatly to making your team the best it can be. If you help your workers develop plans for acquiring healthy self-esteem, you'll create more confident and successful employees. Your team members will learn to accept personal responsibility for themselves, and they'll give and take credit for jobs well done, thus producing a culture of support and encouragement. All of this will also help them bounce back when they face challenges in their work and in their lives.

Like Josee, confident employees are happy to take on new projects and experiences. Supporting them in their learning brings great rewards to everyone.

~ 7 ~

Crate Restrictions: Self-Limiting Behaviours

Holding onto outdated beliefs can restrict your success.
Letting go of them can help you achieve your goals.

I first saw Josee in a photo on Kijiji … her sparkling brown eyes, her smile, and her little "flying nun" ears, as Mark calls them, sitting perkily on her head. I looked at the ad several times before I responded, yet something about that remarkable little puppy made me keep coming back to her.

It wasn't long before Mark and I were driving to an address about 20 minutes from our place and knocking on the door. Josee was a vibrant puppy, and at the time, she was doing a high-energy run around the house. She was an inquisitive little thing with a black coat; a small, white marking on her chest; and an engaging personality to match her adorable face. Mark and I were captivated, and it wasn't long before we were making the trip back to pick her up. We also learned that our new pet was crate trained—that is, she was accustomed to living in her crate while her owner was away.

To bring Josee home with us, we paid two hundred dollars. For that sum, we got a cute dog, a crate, a couple of plastic bowls, a leash, and some food. Even now as I write this, I wonder if I paid for Josee and the crate was free or if I paid for the crate and the dog was free.

When we arrived at our home, she was subdued but still curious—trotting around the house to inspect her new dwelling. We learned right away that she was a food-motivated puppy. It seemed that she would sell her soul for a scrap of something to eat, and this healthy appetite soon sent her into a growth spurt. Before I knew it, she had become so large that her crate seemed to have shrunk overnight. By the time she was eight months old, she had outgrown her sleeping quarters and could no longer stretch out completely until I let her out in the morning.

Because of my demanding schedule, a week went by before I found time to go to the pet store to purchase a new crate. For the first few days, Josee could still stretch a bit in her sleeping chamber, but as the week wore on, she had more and more difficulty stretching out completely. Finally, she realized that she couldn't splay her legs out much at all, and this belief became firmly entrenched in her mind.

Since Josee was part black Lab, I thought she'd continue to grow and expand for some time. I can also be quite frugal and didn't want to go to the expense of purchasing a third crate. The result was that I decided to purchase an extra-large one. This crate is so big that Josee can lie sideways in it, fully extended. She could even do circus acts in there if she wanted to.

The challenge is that despite her roomy new crate, Josee has held onto the belief that she just can't stretch in it. Over a year later, she is still of this opinion. Every day, after she gets out of her nighttime abode, she takes so much time to stretch that she appears to be thinking, "I don't know how I managed to stay in that small space for soooo long."

Josee is now set in her belief that there's no room to stretch out in her extra-large crate, so she never even tries to anymore. To her mind, her crate will always be too small and confining.

As people, we can be a lot like Josee, holding onto beliefs that can be limiting and transferring them to another situation, where they are not appropriate. When this happens, we are often unaware that our viewpoint doesn't fit the new context. This limited perception of the new situation influences how we choose to interact with others, but if we're still "in our old crate," those perceptions will not be accurate. It's easy to hang onto old perspectives, since most of us have subconscious views that impact our daily behaviour. This means that these thoughts govern our actions, though we may not even be aware of them. However, when these inappropriate viewpoints are transferred into the workplace, co-workers and the individual who holds the beliefs can become very frustrated.

I have worked with many team members over the years who have challenges in their relationships, whether personal or professional. I've noticed that these individuals are often baffled as to the "cause" of their problems and may even view them as someone else's responsibility. In situations like this, I asked clients this question: "What is the common theme or commonality in each of these situations?" This would help them become more self-aware and realize how their behaviour was affecting those around them—loved ones and co-workers alike. Once the individual came to understand how their beliefs, thoughts, and behaviours were affecting others, change could happen. Beliefs like this may have been created early in life in response to situations that arose at that time, but they are often no longer effective or relevant, and they may prevent us from seeing our options.

People who have grown up in dysfunctional families are extremely prone to this problem. Dysfunction occurs when family members aren't allowed to feel their emotions, so they don't talk about what's really bothering them. As a result, they don't trust themselves or others. Their internalized belief is that it is not safe to share their opinions, since they will be ostracized or experience other negative consequences if they do that. In an unstable family environment, a person may be less likely to speak up than someone in a well-adjusted family, since their physical and emotional safety may be at risk if they express themselves.

So in a dysfunctional family situation, lack of expression can serve an important, protective function. But if a person takes this set of beliefs and behaviours to the workplace, they will have trouble becoming a fully functioning team member because they may not express their viewpoint when it would be beneficial to do so.

Shelley had such a belief system. She thought it would not be safe to tell her husband, from whom she had been separated for years, that she was in another relationship and had no plans to return to the marriage. According to her internal beliefs, she felt that it was vital not to speak important truths because if she did, something bad might happen or someone else might be upset by what she shared. She transferred this viewpoint to her workplace and would choose to keep secrets and remain silent in order to keep the peace. The environment where she worked was a pleasant, cooperative place, where each team member was encouraged to share their thoughts about the work being done. But Shelley's internal belief was so strong that she still didn't speak up.

As a result of this silent behaviour, she prevented herself and her team from moving forward on one project. Her input could have helped others see potential challenges resulting from the implementation of their plans. But instead of sharing her critical insights, she withheld them, and her team therefore experienced the delays and problems that she had foreseen.

Shelley's belief prevented her team from adapting the project to address her critical thoughts and concerns. Had the team been aware of these observations, they could have become more innovative in their approach, and in the final analysis, their project would have been carried out more successfully.

Have you received feedback from others, either verbal or non-verbal, that one of your beliefs does not fit a certain situation? You can tell that this is happening if you are getting the same or similar feedback from multiple sources. You may notice a pattern of emotion or behaviour that arises for you in a number of relationships—with friends, family, your spouse, or your co-workers. If this is the case, then take time to look at the common denominator. An underlying belief is likely locking you into this thought pattern.

It's vital that you uncover your belief system. One way to do this is to journal your experiences. As you write down what is bothering you and use the word "because" in a sentence, the information that follows is often a hidden belief. For example, Shelley could have written, "I cannot tell others my opinions at work because they won't listen to me." This shows one of her core beliefs: that no one will listen to her. Going another level below this and asking "Why?" may also help expose a more deeply held and deeply hidden belief. As you uncover these beliefs, you can begin to ask yourself about evidence that would prove this was true. Shelley did this with her therapist and later found that she *could* speak up at work and that people listened and used her feedback to ensure success in projects.

Like Shelley, you may be stuck in a way that is preventing you from perceiving the options available in a given situation. Whether or not you realize this is happening, it is important, as a professional, to begin to uncover your underlying beliefs. They have enormous effect on the way you operate. Ask yourself:

- Do I have a common pattern of behaviour that is not effective for me?
- Do I routinely see situations from a fearful perspective?
- What is the fear?
- When do I first remember having the fear?
- When did this fear become one of my beliefs?
- What was happening in my life at the time?

Now look at the situations in your life that have been part of your common pattern. Ask yourself, "Does this belief really fit the current situation?" If you decide it does not, are you willing to release it and let it go? What would be the benefits of letting it go? How would it strengthen you as a person and as a team member?

As a manager or supervisor, you can ask similar questions of your employees, being careful to respect the information that is shared and to keep it in complete confidence. Remember also to assure any employee who talks with you about these issues that you will keep the information in confidence. Although a belief may not fit a situation entirely, it would have been created for a valid reason at the time it came into being. With care and respect, people could be asked to keep a journal about the common struggles they have in relationships at work. By asking them to keep a journal and giving them the questions to ask themselves, you will be providing them with a wonderful tool to help them in many contexts. This process can empower them to understand, from a deeper perspective, the situation they are currently in and other situations that arise later in life.

Of course, everyone brings their internal beliefs to work. After all, wherever we go, our minds and viewpoints are always with us. That is part of being a human being, but the challenge is to become aware of these beliefs so that we are not ruled by old ones that are no longer beneficial. If you continue holding onto old beliefs that do not fit a given situation, you'll be like Josee and not "stretch out" to your greatest potential.

So take the time to understand what beliefs are propelling your behaviours. Then, as you uncover them, check to make sure that they truly are congruent with your current situation and environment. As you work on the beliefs that no longer apply, you'll have much more success in your personal relationships and with your teammates at work.

Unlike Josee, you have the ability to change your beliefs, and this will allow you to become a great supervisor, manager, or team member. Don't "crate yourself" by holding onto outdated belief systems.

~ 8 ~

Outdated Behaviour:
Making Critical Changes

*By developing self-awareness about your behaviour,
you'll be able to adjust to changing circumstances.*

One morning when Josee and I were walking, it was so cold that my jeans felt attached to my legs and created a slight burning sensation. I was wrapped up, but my exposed face was freezing. We were walking quickly because of the cold, and I had only a few minutes before a meeting. As I looked ahead, I could see another dog and its owner heading towards us, and when they came up beside me, Josee immediately engaged with the other dog by jumping up, putting her feet in the other dog's face, and generally taking an aggressive stance. The other dog reacted to Josee's attempt to play by growling, and the growl was not the amicable kind. I needed to get moving and walked away with Josee. As I continued to walk along, I reflected on the interaction between the dogs, admittedly with a little frustration, because I've always wanted Josee to play well with other dogs.

I was almost home when I had a major "Aha!" moment. I realized that Josee was using Great Dane style to engage in play. She'd been spending most of her time playing with our friend's Great Dane, Timothy, and this was the way he interacted. Many breeds of dogs feel overpowered and intruded upon if another dog stands up and puts its paws in their face. To them, this is an aggressive act. They will then react according to their disposition—either shying away if they're passive or attacking if they're dominant.

When I realized this, I became less frustrated with Josee. She'd simply been trying to play with this other dog. She just didn't realize that transferring Great Dane play style to an unknown breed wouldn't bring the results she desired.

People often transfer behaviour patterns from one situation to another as well. After all, we are who we are, and we need to be authentic. However, in the workplace and other such environments, it's important to act in ways that are appropriate to the situation. When we transfer an inappropriate behaviour into the workplace, major challenges can result. For example, if you went to work and acted as if you were on the soccer field, you'd likely get a negative reaction. In fact, we can get so stuck in old behaviours that we can't see other potential ways of acting that could create better outcomes.

When we're stressed, we're more likely to resort to old, ineffective coping strategies. Our minds work less effectively, we become more reactive, and then we may revert to behaviour we used in previous situations in an attempt to reduce the stress. Unfortunately, these very behaviours often increase our stress because of the consequences they create.

When Ed first began work, he transferred a personal coping strategy from childhood into his professional life, and this produced strong feelings of distrust and dislike from co-workers. As a younger brother, he had little power in the family system. He was frequently being told what to do, how to do it, and when to do it. Not just by his parents, but also by his older brother, who was a bully. Ed frankly felt less than an equal in almost any situation, so he learned to observe his older brother's behaviour. When his bossy brother broke a rule, Ed had found a way to get even with him—by reporting these indiscretions to his parents.

As a result, Ed developed the lifelong ability to be very observant of others. As a child, he would use this strong coping strategy to notice what his brother was up to, and then he'd share the information with his parents. Ed would often consider himself to be the family spy, assisting his parents, but he was really the family rat or tattler.

Engaging in this behaviour gave him a sense of power. His parents would listen intently to what he was saying and would believe him. For that brief second, he would feel superior—for him, it was a truly amazing feeling—one he loved! He would hold onto this powerful feeling until the moment he was alone with his older brother, who would bully him more for ratting him out. Despite this undesirable consequence, the initial feeling of power was so appealing that he would tolerate the harassment that came later.

When Ed got his first job, he sometimes felt that his co-workers were slacking off and perhaps taking credit for other people's accomplishments. He would then go to the boss to discuss his concerns. He did not consider himself to be tattling. To his mind, he was merely trying to improve the work situation and felt he had the insight to do so. As you can well imagine, this did not make him a popular co-worker. In fact, his colleagues started to distrust him, and his fan list was quickly dwindling to nil. The amount of stress that he experienced because of this childhood coping strategy was extreme: he was experiencing severe heartburn and was developing an ulcer.

He was not proud of this behaviour, and it took him a few incidents before he realized how this old, outdated way of coping was impacting him and his co-workers. Team members were suspicious of Ed, and this didn't bring him any allies. Even supervisors were frustrated with his behaviour.

Once Ed realized this was an ineffective coping strategy for an adult, and once he understood the true impact of the behaviour, he decided to stop it and change. During moments of stress, when he would contemplate tattling, he would create a different internal dialogue for himself so that he would abstain from old habits. What Ed really desired was to be respected and included as part of the team and to be invited to team activities.

Ed's supervisor was also upset with his behaviour. Although it was probably helpful in one way (since she got to know what was really happening in the team), from a larger perspective, it was simply inappropriate to be acting this way at work. Ed was told to be direct with his co-workers when concerns arose for him, although dealing directly was not one of his strengths. To this day, Ed is grateful that his boss gave him the gift of honest feedback that day.

What can you do if one of your team members is gossiping about other employees? Just as the supervisor did in the example above, it's best to ask that staff member to speak directly to the other employee or employees and to resolve the concerns directly.

To help your gossiping team member process this old behaviour and make changes, ask them questions like the following:

- What prevents you from speaking directly to your co-worker about your concern?
- What were you thinking and feeling before you engaged in this behaviour?
- What are your fears around this situation?
- What do you believe about the current situation?
- Have you ever acted this way in the past?
- Is this an old *pattern* of behaviour (that is, you've done this more than a few times)?
- In the past, how has this pattern of behaviour affected your life?
- How is this pattern working for you or not working for you?
- How might you deal differently with this situation?
- What can you learn from this situation to help you in your future career?
- What might be the payoffs of taking the risk to engage in the new behaviour?

- Are you willing to deal differently with situations like this?

Essentially, you will be asking your employee what their motive is and what outcome they desire. Then you can ask them how they might approach the situation in a new way that will help them achieve their desired outcome. Spend time helping your team member identify a more effective strategy. To make sure your employee doesn't become discouraged or alienated, don't forget to acknowledge that most of us become stuck in old behaviours at various points in our lives. This will normalize the struggle that often comes with behaviour change. At the same time, help your employee realize that you will no longer support tattling, gossiping, or other inappropriate behaviour.

If the employee tries to engage you in this behaviour again, simply remind them of your previous agreement. Then ask them about their situation:

- Are you feeling stressed?
- What is within your control (your thoughts, feelings, and behaviour)?
- What is beyond your control?

Help your team member focus on what they can do themselves to improve the situation. Ask, "What is it about you as a person that causes you to react in this way?" Help them look at their beliefs and behaviour. It's possible that some of that behaviour is being reflected back by the person's co-worker. Little in life is more frustrating than discovering that another person is engaging in behaviour that you personally abhor about yourself. This can cause even the most calm, rational individual to become frustrated and irritated with another person.

Some workplaces have invoked a standard of behaviour stating that no employee is allowed to speak about another employee unless that second worker is in the room at the time. This creates a no-gossip environment, and it helps people to either be direct and honest or, at the very least, to avoid creating drama by gossiping.

As a supervisor or manager, you will find that your employees will struggle with this rule from time to time, so it's essential to keep the rule alive and well. Ensure that you are a solid role model by never speaking negatively about your boss, colleagues, or workers. Help any gossiping employee to see what is causing their frustrations. Perhaps the person is simply feeling overstressed or is struggling with an issue outside of work that is affecting the way they view their co-worker.

By asking questions, you'll be able to identify each individual worker's needs and what behaviours they tend to engage in when stressed. Then you'll be able to find the best ways to support them as they refocus on things that are under their control. This can help them feel empowered, and they will therefore be more likely to deal directly with the situation. This, in turn, will reduce their stress and allow them to get back to the work at hand.

As you come to understand the needs of each employee, you'll be able to treat them in the manner that works best for them while ensuring that each employee is treated equally, albeit uniquely. Your team will then know that you value them and that you see them as capable of dealing with challenges as they arise. This will create a team environment of respect, honesty, and cooperation.

By following this approach, you'll also nurture an environment where all team members will show respect and give each other support as they deal directly with any differences. These straightforward interactions will also save valuable time and energy. In a cooperative workplace like this, your employees will be more relaxed and energetic, and they'll be motivated to become the best team members they can be.

Our Leadership

~ 9 ~

How to Play with the Big Dogs

Learn how to communicate effectively with people at all levels in the company: it's a key to success.

At one dog park I've gone to, I've seen dog bigotry in action. That is, one dog made a snap judgement based on her perception of another one before learning anything about the other dog. The bigot was small—about the size of a Kleenex box. She growled at Josee, who was significantly larger, approached with her teeth bared and her hair bushed out. Then the tiny canine stood up on her back legs and snapped at Josee. The aggressor's owner just smiled and said, "Don't mind her. My dog reacts to larger dogs"—as if to say that the pooch's reaction was cute. Meanwhile, Josee had taken in all the wrath of the Kleenex-box dog. Clearly, the little dog was overcompensating for its lack of size by trying to bite first and ask questions later. She had no interest in learning more about Josee. She simply wanted to be left alone to sniff the beautiful green grass, to be doted on by her owner, and to eventually be picked up and carried home.

Small dogs are not alone in their size prejudice. I've seen medium-sized and large dogs engage in this type of discrimination as well. Timothy, my friend's Great Dane, dislikes smaller dogs and specifically poodles. He has an aversion to them simply because of their size and their hairstyle. It's classic: you are different from me, you have different status, and I don't understand what you need and why you act the way you do. So based on his snap judgement, Timothy is not open to experiencing the benefits of playing with these dogs. They are simply not his size or stature. He takes no time to approach or learn about the other dog.

This type of behaviour can play out in the office in the form of workers who get stuck in their own experience and don't take the time to understand individuals at other levels of the organization. Some workers automatically mistrust managers or supervisors, and some managers or supervisors discount the opinions of front-line workers. The snap judgements happen, and they prevent collaboration at all levels of the organization.

As a team member, do you have difficulty playing with individuals of different statures? Are you intimidated by your boss? Or as a manager or supervisor, do you have difficulty appreciating your workers' skills? It is important to be open to understanding the needs, wants, desires, and responsibilities of others throughout the organization in order to create an environment of collaboration.

As a supervisor, you are responsible for understanding the needs of your manager and also for supporting the needs of your team members. Often, the priorities of the two levels conflict, which may make it difficult for you to reconcile them. However, your ability to balance these two sets of priorities is key to your success. Learning to value the needs of people at each level of the organization without losing sight of your own needs will help you effectively make requests and address concerns as they arise in the workplace.

Every level in the organization has different areas of focus. This is what makes a business successful.

- The Senior Management Team (made up of the Board of Directors and the CEO, the CFO, and other executives) has a forward focus—about three to five years in the future. Their task is to create the vision and direction that will sustain the company over time. They must also ensure that all necessary resources are available to turn the vision into reality.

- The Upper Management Team has a planning scope of about one to three years. They concentrate on making sure that the company's products and services are better than those offered by the competition. They distribute resources internally to the right departments, so that other employees can make superior products and provide top-level services.
- Middle Managers are responsible for three-month to one-year planning and for managing projects on an effective timeline. Their managers create the plans; middle managers have to implement them, using the resources allotted in their budgets.
- Front-Line Supervisors or Managers have a short-term focus: up to three months. They are responsible for ensuring that their team has a clear concept of the plan and of what is expected to be completed within this timeframe. In this way, they ensure that their staff turns the vision of the Upper Management Team into reality.
- The Front-Line Team is responsible for completing tasks, and they generally need to pay attention to daily or weekly responsibilities.

As a supervisor or middle manager, you cannot afford to be intimidated by the larger "dogs." If you are, you won't be able to work with your managers effectively, and you won't be able to address the challenges your team members are experiencing. When your manager makes a demand of your team, how can you better understand her key priorities? What happens if your team is swamped with other projects and simply doesn't have the time to work on the new assignment? How do you effectively approach a situation like this? It's vital that you tell your manager where your own team is at and what its current challenges are. And the way you communicate these points will determine your success or failure.

When you are about to interact with individuals at a higher level in the organization, it will be helpful to ask yourself the following questions:

- What is my objective?
- What outcome would I like to achieve?
- Am I clear about what I will be requesting?
- What information do I require that I do not currently have?
- How might I get the background information that I need to communicate effectively?
- What are the *ongoing* priorities of the manager(s) I'm approaching?
- What is the *current* focus of the manager or managers I'm approaching?
- How might I connect with my manager(s) to understand where they are at?
- What are *my* current priorities and focus? How will these interact with the current priorities of the manager(s) I am dealing with?
- How will my current priorities and focus impact the projections and goals of my manager's or managers' portfolio(s)?
- How can I make my request in a concise manner?
- How might I organize my thoughts so they will make sense from the perspective of the manager(s) I am approaching?

Taking the time to answer the above questions will arm you with the information you'll need to interact with others at all levels of your organization in an effective and articulate way. Once you've addressed these issues, start thinking about how the individual or individuals you'll be speaking with prefer(s) to receive information. Do they like facts? Do they prefer opinions? Or do they need to ask a lot of questions? Some managers will want a written report with statistics and the financial outlook that they can review and respond to. Others may want you to provide them with a list of pros and cons for each potential solution. Still others may have a conversational style, where they want to take the time to discuss the situation and ask you questions.

Learning the preferred style of interaction will help you communicate more successfully with the big dogs. Taking the time to make requests in their particular style makes it easier for them and therefore sets you up for successful interactions. Using this approach, you're likely to overcome any negative preconceptions the "big dogs" may have about "little dogs."

Jim, a social services worker I know, once did preparations like those described above in order to understand the priorities of his manager. As part of his job, Jim had to make assessments that would influence decisions about whether or not to give special assistance to people in financial crisis. One person asking for assistance had been laid off from her job after many years, her unemployment insurance had run out, and she was having great difficulty paying her bills. The client had to choose between paying for groceries for that month or paying a utility bill. After many months of an active job search, she had finally found another job despite the poor economy.

Jim felt that this woman's request for assistance would be a "one-time only" matter—partly because the woman was clearly embarrassed that life had taken her to this level. The challenge for Jim was twofold. First, he knew his manager would likely feel that the woman was trying to take advantage of Social Services. Secondly, given the woman's financial investments (not liquid cash), she was not technically eligible for assistance. Yet Jim truly believed that a small payment would set the woman up for success. So as he sat and strategized, he made the decision to approach his manager to discuss this case.

Jim's manager was the type of person who preferred to be given the facts up front, along with the challenges related to any given situation. As Jim discussed the woman's circumstances with his manager—in her preferred communication style—the manager made the decision to assist this woman so she could pay the utility bill and also buy the groceries she needed.

If you're intimidated by your manager's stature, you'll need to overcome this fear so you can do your job more effectively. This will allow you to be a good communicator instead of falling into the trap of being the little dog that snarls first. As you're thinking about any fears you may have related to the big dogs, remember that no matter what level of job anyone has, we are all human—and that includes your supervisor or manager. He or she is a person just as you are. To put things in perspective, ask yourself, "How did I get my current position? Was it because of my skills and abilities?" Most likely, the answer will be yes. Remember that you have valid input to provide. It's also important to take a few deep breaths just as you are approaching the conversation. Always remember to breathe. It can also be beneficial to create a mantra such as "I have valuable information to share that has merit for the organization" or "People generally listen to and value what I have to say." Repeat that mantra to yourself to overcome your discomfort.

Also make a list of your positive qualities and qualifications—with paper and pen or at your computer. Visualize the conversation flowing, and picture your manager receiving your comments with respect. Remember that all the roles we play in life can have unpleasant and challenging facets, and some aspects of your role may be areas of personal growth for you. Finally, ask yourself, "Is my request or comment important to the success of the company?" If not, it would be best not to proceed. If so, then go for it! But keep your manager's preferred style in mind.

As a middle manager or supervisor, you must at the same time ensure that you are effectively managing your team. Are your employees truly using their time as effectively as possible? Are they on board with the team's priorities? Do they know how to prioritize their tasks appropriately? Are they becoming sidelined by other tasks that are not vital at this time? (These strategies will be covered in Chapter 18.)

By learning to overcome any discomfort you may have in dealing with people at all levels of your organization, you will become a stronger supervisor or manager, and you'll be able to pass these communication skills on to your team members. You'll be able to play with "dogs" of all statures.

Don't be like Timothy, who is not open to poodles!

~ 10 ~

Alpha Dog Leadership

In the dog park, alpha dogs know their strength
as leaders of the pack. Team leaders also need to be aware
of their strengths—and weaknesses.

My massage therapist, Lynne, once told me the story of how she acquired Bo, her Terrier cross. He'd come from Mississippi, a rescue dog brought to Canada after a hurricane that devastated the southern U.S. a few years ago. First, he went to a foster home. Then Lynne adopted the Terrier—a gorgeous, well-mannered blond.

Bo's foster home was in the country, about an hour and a half away from Lynne's place, so she had an easy drive when she and her husband headed out there one fine spring day to pick up her new pet. Bo's foster home was a brick farmhouse at the end of a driveway flanked by huge, old maple trees. There was an old-style wooden barn behind the house, and maple trees stood all around the barnyard.

As Lynne parked her car, the breeder came out of the house with several dogs in tow to greet the visitors. Most of the dogs were approaching Lynne and her husband, seeking attention and persistently trying to be petted. But the smallest dog of the pack was unique. He sidled up with an aloof attitude, sniffed Lynne, and then, with a confident stride, walked away and into the barnyard. The other dogs stayed behind, still trying to get the attention of their guests. All of a sudden, the smallest dog, clearly the alpha dog of the pack, trotted up to the top of a slight hill in the barnyard and made a barking-growling sound. All the other dogs immediately stopped their attention-seeking activities and ran to the alpha dog. There was no hesitation. They all knew that the leader of the pack had spoken and that it was their job to follow the leader.

After a few minutes, the dogs ambled over to the barn, where they helped themselves to bones from a bin. The alpha dog ate first, followed by the next strongest dog, and so on. In the dog world, the leader of the pack is chosen because of its strength. This makes sense, since the leader has the responsibility of making sure that the pack survives. At some point, this alpha dog would have clearly communicated his strength and virility to the other dogs. He also had the intelligence to make sure that the pack would survive. Knowing his abilities, the other dogs had accepted him as their leader.

In the human realm, it's not always as clear why someone becomes a supervisor or manager. At times, the decision is not based on merit alone. A leader may be chosen because of seniority or because of who they know versus what they know. They may know the manager personally or even be related. They may be promoted for other reasons despite having limited leadership abilities. But in the dog-eat-dog world of the workplace, team members may reject a new manager or supervisor who's been appointed for reasons other than ability, precisely because they do not possess the qualities required to be a good leader.

As a result of these hiring practices, it is possible to be supervised by someone who is less competent as a leader than you are. Skilled front-line workers are sometimes promoted because of their expertise in their work, even though they lack the skills of a solid leader. Some supervisors and managers may pick favourites and manage by emotion as opposed to doing what is best for the team. If such practices were followed in the dog world, canines would likely have been extinct years ago as a result of infighting, inability to recognize threats to the pack, and lack of focus on priorities (finding food and shelter and fending off attackers).

In one workplace, the manager, Jerry, was incredibly unpredictable. One day she would pass team members in the hall and totally ignore them, and the following day, she would act as if the same person was her best friend—joking and being playful with them. The day after that, she might be angry with that same person for no apparent reason. There was no clear cause and effect that anyone could determine about her moods.

One day, Beth arrived at the office and received a message that her father-in-law had passed away. She was upset and needed to go home to support her husband but wanted to let someone in management know what was happening. Jerry was the only manager who was in, so Beth proceeded to her office, waiting patiently outside her door as Jerry finished a phone call. When she hung up, Jerry yelled at Beth and told her to go away because she was busy. Emotionally overwhelmed, Beth sought out a co-worker, explained the situation, and asked him to tell their supervisor when he arrived that she'd had to go home to be with her husband.

Jerry had incredible computer skills and could solve any computer problem with ease. She'd been given the position because of her ability to fix difficult technical issues. But when it came to people skills, Jerry was sorely lacking.

A skilled manager, who is self-aware, is able to put aside his or her own moods to address an employee in a caring and respectful way. That morning, Beth had needed only one minute of Jerry's time. Instead of yelling at Beth, she could have asked what she needed while still letting her know that she was busy—but in a respectful tone. Beth could then have told Jerry the situation quickly and been on her way.

If you've been promoted to a leadership position or to a higher-management position, you may need to learn some new skills. As a manager or supervisor, you'll need to develop an understanding of how to motivate your team members while being flexible, fair, and objective with everyone.

Here are some questions you can ask yourself as you're moving into your role as supervisor or manager. Even if you're already an experienced manager or supervisor, you may gain some insights from your answers to these questions that will help you improve your skills.

- What methods do I use to inspire my team?
- What are my greatest competencies in positively influencing my employees?
- How could I improve my motivational skills?
- Do I operate from a place of integrity? That is, are my personal values based on fairness, respect, and consideration? Are my actions congruent with the values I say I have?
- Do I give credit where credit is due—to both my workers and my superiors?
- Am I enthusiastic about my work? Do I communicate this enthusiasm in order to encourage my team?
- Do I communicate clearly—both verbally and non-verbally? Does this clarity increase my team's confidence?
- Do I assert myself when needed?
- Am I willing and able to confront challenges directly and with respect?
- Do I correct employees in private so that they may save face in relation to their fellow employees?
- Do I work towards my goals or company objectives, knowing what it takes to achieve them?
- Do I actively work to help my employees excel and rise to new levels in the organization?
- Am I committed to excellence in all that I do?
- How do I deal with disappointment? How do I overcome strong emotions so that they don't negatively affect my team members?

Skilled supervisors and managers lead by example, respect their team members, listen to their employees' needs and desires, and help their staff members understand their roles on the team. They even acknowledge and deal with their own shortcomings as leaders. When a leader is fair, thoughtful, and respectful and has good interpersonal communication skills, others will want to follow their lead.

Good leaders can strategize based on the big picture and also forecast how a situation may impact team members. They are self-aware and realize how their interactions affect other people. A solid leader takes the time to understand each employee, learning what motivates them and how to communicate in order for the employee to truly hear what is being said. Understanding that each employee is a unique individual and balancing this perception with fair and equitable treatment of all team members are hallmarks of a stellar leader.

If you are currently a supervisor or manager, think about the leadership skills you already have and the skills that you lack. Are you able to articulate this for yourself? If not, you may need to obtain feedback from both superiors and workers to ensure that you're reading your skills accurately. Understanding where you're at now will enable you to identify your learning and growth needs. Then you'll be able to create a plan to grow in areas of lack while maintaining or improving your strengths.

If you decide to ask others to give you feedback about your strong points and areas of growth, you might want to use an Internet tool that helped a colleague of mine. She was on a Board of Directors with me, and she asked a number of people (including me) to give her feedback: her managers, her clients, colleagues at previous workplaces, and past colleagues such as myself. When I signed on, I was able to rate her on the items on which she wanted feedback. All comments were then collated by the software and presented as anonymous feedback to her—all within the context of a questionnaire she'd set up that addressed a new skill set she'd been working on.

Once you become more aware of your strengths and weaknesses as viewed by others, you can take the time to integrate this information and create a plan of action to improve. Your plan may include reading books on the subject, taking additional courses, and finding a mentor or coach to become the best leader you can be. As your management skills increase, you'll be able to motivate your employees more effectively and help them grow into their potential.

In the dog world, leaders are strong, and they're focused on the long-term survival of the pack. Humans would be smart to follow their example.

~ 11 ~

Achieving a Common Goal with Strategy

*Effective strategizing can improve
your team's chances of success enormously.*

For the last four years, Mark and I have been building our cottage ourselves. Surrounded by tall cedars and a few birches, it's a perfect location for a retreat, but so far, it's largely been a labour camp. Last summer, however, we'd progressed to the point that we had some time off while we waited for a contractor to finish the drywall. So we decided to take advantage of the break to just enjoy our partially built abode, and one day we invited our friends Catherine and Mitchell—and their dog Timothy—to join us for a weekend.

As they arrived on Saturday morning and got out of their vehicle, Josee was over the moon with excitement as her buddy Timothy jumped out of the SUV. They instantly went into play mode, Timothy being even more enthusiastic than usual, since he'd been cooped up in the SUV for the long drive.

After lunch, Mark and Mitchell left to do an errand, and Catherine and I went inside the cottage with the dogs. Catherine is one of the kindest, most thoughtful people I know. Being a busy consultant, she had just finished a hectic week at the office and needed time to chill out. The dogs had lain down quietly while we were eating lunch, but now they were rested and ready to play with a vengeance. We decided to do the dishes, but the dogs were making so much noise as they played tug and bumped into the side table in the living room that we couldn't hear ourselves think let alone have a conversation. So we put the dogs outside.

Timothy and Josee were thrilled. Before long, they were wrestling on the front lawn, having a splendid time. We left them to their entertainment, thinking we'd soon be able to relax and have a nice, cold drink on the deck after the dishes were washed.

Then, just when we were about to put our dish towels away, we heard a high-pitched ^{whine} followed a few seconds later by a WROOF. A moment later, there was another ^{whine} followed by another WROOF and so on as the dogs took turns asking to be let inside the cottage. Catherine and I listened in amazement at this expertly coordinated display of canine communication.

Their timing was impeccable. After a few minutes of listening to this expertly planned duet and despite our desire to relax, we gave in and let the dogs back into the cottage. They trotted right past us, tails wagging, knowing they'd got their way.

It appeared clear to me that in some way, Josee and Timothy had communicated a shared goal: to get back into the cottage. Then they'd come up with a strategic plan, which they'd implemented with superb skill. They'd identified their individual roles and played them well as they orchestrated their way to success.

Timothy and Josee's clever scheme can be applied almost directly to team practices. When a team spends the time to create clear objectives, strategizes to create a plan based on those objectives, and then diligently implements the plan, great productivity and achievements will result.

You could say that the two canines used a four-step process to create and implement their plan to get back into the cottage. If you put it in a table, it would look like this:

Determine goal	Brainstorm solutions	Create road map	Assign tasks/ Implement master plan
Get inside the cottage	Scratch door, bark, whine, throw body against the door, put paws up on window ledge and look in with sad eyes	Start barking at lake edge, increase frequency of bark as we get closer to cottage, alternate whines and barks at the door	Josee to whine, followed by Timothy's WROOF

The process you and your team members will be using to strategize and reach your goal will be more sophisticated, of course, but the four steps are similar: (1) determine your goal and decision-making processes, (2) brainstorm solutions, (3) create a road map and assign tasks, and (4) implement your master plan.

1. Determine your goal and decision-making processes

First, decide what the goal is. There are many possible ways of making this decision, and some are better for team functioning than others. Here are three types of decision-making structures you can use:

a. *Consensus* decision making gives all team members input in a cooperative manner. It also results in a decision that all team members can support, either because they agree fully with the goal or because they understand the reason for the goal and the beliefs or values that make the goal important. As the goal is arrived at in a collaborative way, it's more likely to be supported by all employees.

One of the challenges of this style is that it's often time consuming, because all staff members need to be able to state their opinions. However, participants in the discussion will realize that they are all being treated equally and that everyone has a valued point of view.

b. The *voting decision-making process* involves having a discussion about all aspects of the goal, followed by each team member voting for their preference. The goal voted for by the majority will be the one chosen. While this model is less time consuming, it may cause some team members to feel they've failed, since they didn't "win" the vote. Those team members may therefore be less committed to the goal.

c. *Top-down decisions* occur when management decides to create a particular goal and then tells the staff what the goal is. This method often results in a manager or supervisor needing to get "buy-in" on the goal from their team members. In this case, staff can end up feeling excluded from the process and may not readily offer their support, so as a manager or supervisor, you must help each team member understand the rationale used for the decision. Your employees will then be more likely to get on board with the plan.

Regardless of how you set goals with or for your team, you'll need to make sure that everyone appreciates the rationale behind the decision and links it back to the team's values. This will help your team members engage with the goal, and when they're engaged, they'll be more motivated to go the extra mile to ensure that the project succeeds.

As a manager or supervisor, what can you do when a team member does not support the goal?

- Sit down and have an open discussion about their concerns.
- Encourage them to tell you what aspects of the objective they are struggling with.
- Ask them what part of the goal they *can* support. Start to build from a place of agreement, however small that may be.
- Ask your employee what would have to happen for them to get on board with a decision.

Perhaps the goal conflicts with a moral value such as working on a marketing strategy for a gambling establishment when gambling is against the person's religious beliefs. Ask yourself how you can support the team's goals and the individual's integrity at the same time. Could this person be assigned to a different project or to a different part of the project that has a more general application? Ask the employee how they might be able to complete the tasks required of them without going against their conscience.

2. Brainstorm solutions

The second step is to brainstorm possible ways of reaching the goal. Take the time to explore possibilities with your team so they can reveal their natural creativity. Set a tone of openness in the meeting, instructing your employees to make no criticisms of any idea while the meeting is being held—as some amazing discoveries have come from apparently crazy proposals. Remember to use the "yes and" technique from Chapter 4. It's always helpful to record notes of your team's brainstorming ideas on a flip chart or white board or interactive white board. Sometimes seeing one idea in print can lead to other creative strategies and solutions.

3. Create a road map and assign tasks

Next, let the team create a road map to success, or a master plan, by breaking the larger goal down into manageable segments. Then each team member can decide which parts they want to be involved in based on their strengths and learning goals. Assuming that all the tasks are distributed fairly and that all team members are involved and engaged in the process, you and your team members can then create timelines, giving dates for the completion of each task.

If there is a conflict between two team members who both want to complete the task, help them to negotiate with one another to determine how they might share the task. For tasks that no one wants to do, have a team discussion about who will take them on.

Keep track of who is willing to come forward, to ensure that all team members take turns completing the undesirable tasks. If everyone knows that team members will be taking turns carrying out these functions, all employees will be more likely to step up and do their part.

4. Implement your master plan

To implement the master plan your team has just drawn up, have them give each task a due date that will enable all goals to be reached in a timely way. Your team members will also take on the responsibility of keeping track of timeframes. It may be helpful to have the implementation plan created and posted on the wall or the computer so team members can refer to it easily and update it as items are completed. Let them know that it's their responsibility to get in touch with you as soon as they think there may be difficulty in completing their task on time. Tell them that as struggles arise, they will be free to share them with the team. Assure them that they have a solid supervisor and team behind them to help them through the tough spots.

As a supervisor or manager, you'll need to make sure that your team members have the understanding and the resources required to execute their tasks effectively and on time. Remind them every so often that you're available to support them if needed. Also let your staff know what you mean by "availability." Do you have an open-door policy (that is, when your door is open, you can be interrupted)? Or do you let your staff know what hours you're available? If you're on a different floor, can they email or phone you anytime? If you're clear about your availability, your employees will be empowered, since they'll know exactly when you'll be there to give any necessary guidance or support.

Help your team decide what form of decision-making process fits their personalities and therefore works best for them. Do you have a group that continues to brainstorm and create wonderful ideas but has difficulty moving into action? If so, they may need to shift the decision-making process from a consensus model to a voting model to ensure that the project is completed by the deadline. They could also set a time limit on their brainstorming sessions that will allow them to indulge in their creativity but then move on to the best possible decision without undue delay. At that point, you, as supervisor or manager, will need to make it clear that the team should generate no more ideas and move on to implementation.

Other teams may have the opposite problem: they may want to jump into implementing an idea before exploring other options. In cases like this, take the time to slow your team down and help them by leading a brainstorming session. If idea generation is not their preference, give them a specific amount of time to work on this exercise. Ask them questions like the following:

- How might we overcome this challenge?
- What other options might solve the problem?
- What is the most outrageous solution you can come up with for this challenge? If the sky was the limit and resources were endless, how would you suggest that we reach this goal?

Write down any and all ideas as they arise. Once the team has created a good range of possibilities, help them determine which is the best possible solution, by consensus or by voting, since a top-down decision would have to be made by the supervisor or manager, not by the team collectively.

Your team will thank you for helping them follow these steps in planning and implementation. The whole process will help everyone work within their areas of strength, where they can really shine. Regularly check with your team to see what step they are on and help them stay on track. If they're falling behind, help them revisit the process so their success will be guaranteed. They'll be grateful to you in the end, when they reap the benefits of staying on schedule.

Josee and Timothy had the satisfaction of cooperating and strategizing to reach their goal of getting back into the cottage. Your team will also enjoy a spirit of mutual support and the satisfaction of achievement if you give them the opportunity to create their own strategies and move the project forward using the methods that are most effective for them.

~ 12 ~

To Leash or Not to Leash?

Before "leashing" an employee,
give the process some careful thought.

Four years went by between the time that our last dog, Tiffy, passed away and Josee arrived on the scene. During this period, our neighbours Bill and May brought a beautiful little black furball into their home—an English Lab puppy named Ali. I fell in love. I've watched Ali go through all the stages of development until she became a sleek, stocky adult dog. She has a barrel-shaped midriff that makes some people think she's overweight, but this is just a typical characteristic of an English Lab. She's now a healthy, alert, and attentive dog of about five years.

While other women crave motherhood, I crave puppies. And May knows it, so she kindly gave me honorary puppy privileges. This meant that every morning as I headed out to my car, I'd get a few moments to play with Ali and start my day with a smile. It was difficult to tell who enjoyed these stolen moments more—the pup or me. Ali was always eager to see me, standing up with a wagging tail as I approached. She's the kind of dog you'd want to take home to meet mother: attractive, gentle, and respectful, and she knows her place. Bill trained her so well that she usually doesn't even need a leash.

One lovely summer morning, Josee and I were coming back home after our walk in the park. The sun was already hot, and I knew the day was going to be a scorcher. As we were approaching our place, we bumped into Bill, who was coming along the sidewalk with Ali. Nothing unusual about that—except that Ali was on a leash. I was curious about that, of course, but Bill explained that they were going to a festival a few blocks away, and Ali had to be leashed, as there would be so many people there.

As Bill and I chatted, Josee and Ali sniffed each other in a friendly way. Then, right after they finished wagging their tails at each other, they growled and bared their teeth and raised their hackles. We settled them down, but the transformation was so dramatic that I wondered what had caused it. "Oh, dogs on leash," said Bill. "Honestly, they have no clue what's going on." (When a dog is tethered to a human, it may misread the tightening of the leash as tension, causing it to react to the other dog. As a result, when another dog comes along, it has difficulty reading the new body-language signals and, like Josee when she saw Ali, makes a negative interpretation when the leashed dog meant no harm. This results in the dogs going on the defensive.)

Like dogs on leash, workers who are subjected to excessive, arbitrary, or subjective rules become frustrated. For instance, rules are sometimes instituted to correct the behaviour of only one or a handful of employees, and this tends to alienate and frustrate the 98 percent who don't need the rules to act appropriately and complete their tasks.

One manager, for instance, asked everyone to come to a meeting 15 minutes early because of a few individuals who were chronically late. Meanwhile, the attendees who showed up 10 minutes early for the false 15-minutes-early start time would end up losing 25 minutes that could have been spent working on other pressing projects.

When restrictions like these are arbitrarily put in place for all individuals, those who do not need them feel insulted, frustrated, and often demotivated. Meanwhile, the minority who really need to change their behaviour continue to challenge the rules.

Likewise, people who rarely take a break and work full tilt may legitimately need 20 minutes to clear their minds before moving on to the next task. But these employees may lose out because Bob, the chronic overbreaker, takes 30 minutes off, and management has therefore reduced breaks to 10 minutes. Of course, the hard workers will feel resentful towards Bob and insulted by management.

Rules like this also send the message that you don't trust your employees and they should maybe not trust you either. In an environment like this, normally great workers will begin to cut corners in their work because they don't feel respected by management. It's as if they're saying, "Frank, my manager, doesn't trust me anyway, so why don't I just sneak out early today." As a supervisor or manager, do you want to have your team members respect you? If so, don't put tight leashes on all your employees because one or a few people are causing problems. Deal directly with the unacceptable behaviour as it arises by speaking with the "Bobs" alone, and let your "good majority" keep on doing what they normally do.

In a team setting, frustration and resentment can adversely affect the quality of the work generated. The "Bobs" of this world will just continue to do as little as possible while others are working their fingers to the bone and being punished for someone else's improper behaviour. This style of management is expensive. It's far more costly to the team's functioning than it is to go through the difficult process of addressing Bob directly about his behaviour.

Most supervisors and managers would rather not have to confront their employees about inappropriate behaviour. However, it's essential to overcome any discomfort you might have about addressing performance issues with your staff. The long-term rewards will be worth it. Leave your dedicated employees alone to work on their tasks and give them the freedom they need to use their best work styles. Not all dogs require leashes to behave—even though some will create chaos without one.

Then, if an issue arises, take "Bob" aside and clearly identify where he has violated the established norms of the workplace. Help him understand the impact of his behaviour on his fellow employees and the team. Ask Bob what is causing his behaviour and work with him to make a plan to improve. Ask him if there is something he needs to perform his work more effectively without taking long breaks. Tell him what the consequences will be if he continues to challenge the established rules and policies. Hopefully, Bob will change his behaviour after this, but you may discover that he isn't a good fit with the team culture you've developed. When you have an employee who consistently challenges the rules, negatively impacting their work, you will need to continue to meet with them, document your discussions, and involve Human Resources. It may be necessary to let the employee go.

If you've realized, as you're reading this, that you've set down some rules that are not needed for your 98 percent, consider lifting the restrictions. For example, some managers create complicated processes because some team members don't follow simple processes. As a result, the entire team has to go through multiple steps to accommodate a few employees who don't think their tasks through.

What policies undermine your staff members? How might you alter them as a reflection of appreciation for your team members' hard work? How might this free up emotional energy that your staff could use to work on team goals?

When you create an environment of trust and directly manage breaches to acceptable team behaviour, you'll find that your staff respect you and that they'll be motivated to do more, create more, and generally rise to the challenge of the freedom you've given them.

Even Ali breaks out of the rules every so often. Once, when she saw me across the street, she came running over to see me instead of continuing on her walk with Bill. This has happened only once, and Bill dealt with her directly, respectfully, and clearly so she'd remember that this was unacceptable, unsafe behaviour. As a manager or supervisor, ask yourself whether an employee who breaks a rule is generally a fantastic worker who is having a bad day or whether the issue is chronic. The process may be as simple as asking Joan what's happening for her that day, which may have triggered their uncharacteristic 25-minute break. You may discover that she has just worked nonstop on a crisis for the last three hours and needed to shake it off. Or she may be feeling unwell or may be dealing with a personal crisis.

When your team is aware of what is expected from them, and when they know that you'll deal effectively and directly with problematic performance, they'll feel a sense of relief and will respect you as a manager or supervisor. The internal motivation of an employee who knows that they are respected and valued is exponentially higher than that of an employee who feels as if they've been tied up by a group of rules they never needed.

Just like Josee, who was frustrated by her leash, these motivated team members will work best when they are given a reasonable amount of freedom.

~ 13 ~

Treats and Employee Appreciation

*When you demonstrate appreciation for a job well done,
your team members will become even more dedicated.*

When Josee was in puppy training class, we were encouraged by the trainer to use treats to reward her good behaviour. The pouch I used to hold the treats was open at the top, so when I bent over, some would fall out by mistake and Josee would gobble up the goodies even when she hadn't done a trick or obeyed a command. So I switched to using the left pocket of my coat to hold the treats. Not so easy for Josee, but it means she's more willing to work for her rewards.

Of course, she'd rather munch on these delicacies all the time. In fact, she knows exactly where we keep our permanent stash of treats in a cupboard beside our basement stairs. When the basement door opens, she runs to the cabinet and points her nose towards it and then back towards me. It's as if she's saying, "Just in case you're looking for the treats, they're right here. And oh, yeah, I'd be happy to have one." Josee is only somewhat successful with these blatant hints, and she always has to do some trick or desired behaviour to get her treat. Whether it's a high five, shake a paw, or sit, she knows that treats are earned as a result of good behaviour.

Mark and I have different management styles in the treat-dispensing department, and Josee responds differently to each of us. She knows she has to listen and do specifically what I want to get a treat. Through my firm and consistent treatment of her, she knows that I won't give the treat unless she performs the appropriate task. If I ask her to sit, she cannot lie down to get the treat. She has to sit. I won't respond to any other behaviour.

My husband is a much gentler soul than I am and is more generous in doling out the goodies. I've observed Josee doing a crazy dance for him, trying to anticipate what he wants from her. She'll sit, lie down, roll on her side, and lie down again—all in an effort to figure out what he wants her to do. He thinks it's cute, and I must admit it really makes me laugh to watch her do all these tricks in 10 seconds or less. Because Mark rewards her after this frenzied dance, this is what Josee almost always performs for him. She's not as clear about what's expected of her than when she's working with me, and she's willing to take the reward whether she's truly earned it or not.

Josee is a quick learner. I decided one day to teach her how to "high 5" and broke the trick down into small increments, rewarding her for each small action as we went along. For example, I had to teach her to touch my hand with her paw. When she did that, I rewarded her with verbal praise and a treat. Within 10 minutes, I'd taught her to "high 5" and "Give me 10." She had the innate talent, but she became a star learner when motivated by the delectable doggie morsels and my verbal praise.

What happens in your team when employees do a great job? When they conquer a new challenge, do they receive acknowledgement and praise? Humans aren't so different from dogs in our desire to be recognized for a job well done and in our positive response when we receive that acknowledgement. That's why a well-thought-out employee recognition program can be so important for your employees' morale.

Some people may question this and say, "The feeling of having done a good day's job should be enough encouragement to keep working away." I believe rewards need to be given in a balanced way—not always "falling out of the pocket" like the treats Josee grabbed when she was a puppy, but frequently enough that employees will know their efforts have been noticed. We want employees to value their own work and to have a solid work ethic, but it's equally important to support their endeavours by giving them verbal praise and sometimes even a "treat."

Employee recognition programs can have their down sides, however. Sometimes employees become so focused on receiving the prize that they forget to do their best, just as Josee does with Mark. Some people see themselves as entitled to recognition or they see the rewards as the goal. In one sales company, rewards were given out so liberally that some employees began engaging in unethical activity in order to obtain the big cheque. The reward cheque was based on total sales, and some personnel resorted to purchasing product themselves to falsely inflate their sales levels. They were focusing on getting the prize instead of doing quality work.

Any successful employee recognition program has to be directly linked to the mission and values of the organization. When you do this, it's more likely that the behaviour will be linked with the goal instead of being viewed as a means of obtaining an unearned bonus. This framework also reflects back the reason for the reward: that the individual is creating something of value for the entire team and company through their contribution.

Employee reward programs present other challenges as well. If they have been in place at a company for some time, employees may begin to feel entitled to a reward. For example, at one workplace, each employee traditionally receives a Christmas gift basket and some money at the end of the year. Recently, however, the gift basket had to be cancelled, though the financial rewards were still given. When the employees heard about this, they were upset that they weren't getting their Christmas gift basket—even though the money reward had been increased to cover the value of the gift. The employees felt entitled and would be happy only if they received what they *perceived* they deserved.

All in all, however, well-designed and well-administered employee recognition programs do a great deal to increase employee morale. First, find out what each of your team members would value as a reward. In other words, follow the Platinum Rule (treating others the way they wish to be treated). If you don't have the budget to purchase gifts that would be valued by a high-performing employee, give verbal feedback or send personally written notes. If you have a shy employee, it may be important to give quiet feedback on a one-on-one basis, while another person might want to be addressed publicly in a team meeting. If you do have the budget, find out what your employees like: perhaps one loves coffee and another books. Giving them gift cards that reflect their personal interests will really mean something. Keep a record of who you've acknowledged to make sure you don't show favouritism.

Gifts shouldn't be given as incentives. They need to be true rewards, offered after an employee has done a task or carried out an interaction with great skill. And be sure not to give out rewards as a routine year after year. If you do, your employees may take them for granted. Some employees may pull a Josee and chase after the reward, rather than focusing on the quality of their work and input.

Whenever you acknowledge an employee with a note or a gift, be certain to say exactly what they did. For instance, you could write, "John, the process you created last week saved time for all our salespeople. The chart you developed lets every employee know how close we are to our target and really adds to the teamwork we do here." That would be better than saying, "Good job last week." It is important to link the acknowledgement to the team goals and company mission and values whenever possible. When you focus on the positive and share your observations, you'll find that your team will have a more positive outlook as well.

It's also a good idea to give your employees a few minutes at the weekly team meeting to talk about their "wins" of the week and to thank each other for their contributions. This goes a long way to enhance team dynamics through employee-to-employee recognition, and it's a great method of reinforcing what's working and to encourage more of it.

Just like Josee, team players who receive rewards for specific behaviours at appropriate times will be motivated and positive in their outlook.

~ 14 ~

Inspiring Growth and Development

*Continuous learning and growth promotes
motivated and inspired employees.*

People tell me that Josee is a very intelligent dog. Once, when I was working at the University of Guelph as a Simulated Client, a dog was needed to play the role with me. As a Simulated Client, I play a predetermined role with a student and then offer them feedback about their communication skills. When university staff suggested that Josee should come in to play the dog's role, I remembered that we'd chatted previously about Josee's personality and some of the challenges I was experiencing with her. I was concerned that she might be distracting and therefore spoil the learning opportunity, which was very important to the participating students. As a result, we held an audition for her to see whether she'd be able to relax enough to manage the role. She passed—and she was to play the role of an out-of-control dog that her owner needed help with. Not a total stretch for Josee, given her high energy levels!

As Josee and I entered the classroom at University of Guelph, a veterinary student greeted us, saying, "Hello, would you like to have a seat?" I sat down on a nearby chair. The student spoke with me and then engaged with Josee and then returned to speak with me. Josee lay down and often dosed off to sleep. The priority was to ensure that the students got an opportunity to use their communication skills and to get a good video copy of their interactions so they could review those responses later.

At times, Josee would whine and disrupt the process. I would then escort her out of the room, where a staff member would take over and lead Josee away for a break. Sometimes Josee and her dog sitter would go outside for a walk and sometimes they'd visit with the students who were in the observation room. Josee was in her glory at break time: socializing with groups of up to 20 doting students, going on exciting walks, getting plenty of treats, and generally being the centre of attention. She was soon hooked on the working world. Talk about employee recognition programs: every day she was at the university, she revelled in the appreciation she was getting for her natural talents.

By the third day, she was well into the routine of going to work. In the morning, at least 20 minutes before we needed to leave, she'd be sitting beside the door, waiting to go. She'd look over at me on the couch as if to say, "Hurry up. We've got work to do." She was a dedicated employee—motivated to arrive early at work each day and excited about taking on the necessary tasks. She worked hard, since she had to play at least four scenarios with new students every day. And I believe she derived a sense of accomplishment from what she was doing. It must have been a good workout for her, since back home, after the sessions were over, she'd always have a big, long nap.

Josee received a positive performance review. Well, okay, the program coordinator told me that Josee had done an amazing job given her age, since she'd been able to stay in the room for a good, long time. To my—and, I think, Josee's— delight, she was invited back to do more role-playing work at the university.

Are your team members highly motivated and excited about going to work? Do you have employees on your team who've lost their spark? Perhaps they're bored and no longer feel challenged. And boredom is a dangerous state of mind to have in the workplace. When individuals are uninspired, they don't focus as carefully on their tasks and they tend to work at half mast, putting in the least amount of effort required. When employees are just going through the motions, they need to be given opportunities to learn and grow. This way, they'll be challenged and encouraged to become more enthusiastic and creative. They might even get back the spark they had in the first place.

Your employees are not unlike Josee, who will be highly motivated when they experience appropriate challenge and stimulation. We all have skills that can be developed and areas that we would like to explore. How do you, as supervisor or manager, create opportunities for your workers?

First, get to know your employees so you can help them develop personal goals related to work. Then have them write down their goals, and tell them that you'll be integrating those objectives into the performance appraisal process. At the end of the year, give each team member clear, concise feedback, so you can help them set out areas of growth for the following year. By taking the time to explore the skills and knowledge your team members really want to develop, your performance appraisals will be more relevant to them. And by actively seeking out ways to create learning opportunities for them in these areas, you'll all be rewarded—your employees, your team, and the company.

One manager once told an employee about areas where that worker needed to grow, but the manager didn't take the time to get to know where the employee was truly at in his job at the time. The employee was assigned to new initiatives that other workers would like to have been involved with, but this employee was not so enthused about his new responsibilities. The team member would have been much more motivated if the manager had asked him what areas he wanted to learn more about. Then, together, they could have carved out learning opportunities that would have been relevant to both the employee and the company.

Some team members, however, might not know what goals they'd like to set for learning. So if a worker like this is really stuck, give them some suggestions. Have the employee spend time reflecting on where they want to go within the company and in their career. If a bored, unmotivated employee realizes that they don't want to go anywhere within the company or that they want a different career, a good leader will not try to keep them. It may be best for the employee and your company to help an employee who feels they're in a rut to move to another job.

For most team members, though, you'll be able to settle on two or three annual goals that will make them excited about their jobs. Then together you'll need to find ways to meet those goals. Get your employees involved in finding learning opportunities. First, let them know what you can pay from your department budget. Then make it a team effort to seek out learning opportunities.

The learning opportunities that you and your employees do find could take one of several forms. You could send employees out for specific training that they want, but this can be expensive. However, the payoff is that you'll be bringing fresh ideas and concepts into your department. It's good practice to have the employee offer their fellow team members a session about what they learned at the seminar they attended. This can expand your team member's knowledge in two ways. First, by preparing a presentation, the person who went to the training will have the opportunity to review their learning, thus cementing it in their minds. Secondly, all members of the team will benefit by learning the new information.

If several members of your team have similar learning objectives, you can hire a specialist to come in and train them all together. If budget allows, it would also be good to have the employees go off site for the day, so they can focus on their learning, free of distractions such as voicemail and emails.

If budget is a challenge, you may need to become more creative in finding effective ways to train your staff. Perhaps your employee is so motivated to get a particular kind of training that you can cost-share. For instance, your company could give your team member paid time off, while the team member would pay for the actual seminar. Many employees believe that their employer should be responsible for creating their learning goals and paying for their training. But when an employee funds a portion of the costs, they'll likely be more highly motivated to get the most from the experience.

Another option is to create a mentoring project at your workplace. Have team members shadow each other in their different tasks. Look for individuals in your company who are highly skilled in the area that one of your team members wishes to learn. They could be managers or other employees, and they could act as mentors. You could even have a new employee co-mentor a more experienced employee if the new arrival has skills the more experienced employee would like to learn. For example, a younger employee may have amazing computer skills that they could share with the seasoned employee, while the more senior employee could pass on the benefits of their experience in the business to the newer one. This creates a win-win situation, where everyone is valued and has the opportunity to learn and to teach.

Online learning also presents excellent opportunities. Distance education courses, teleseminars, and webinars may also be less expensive than "in-person" workshops and courses. For employees who don't have their own offices, offer a place in the boardroom for them to take their online course.

Get your employees involved in finding appropriate training. First, let them know what you can pay from your department budget. Then launch a team effort to seek out learning opportunities.

Bored, uninspired employees mean uninspired business for you. So make sure your employees are given opportunities for growth. Then, like Josee, they'll be enthusiastic and motivated. By helping them realize they're in charge of their own learning, you'll create buy-in, and this will help them become more creative in managing their goals.

Team members who are involved in continuous learning and development will know that you value them and that you are open to helping them become the best workers they can be, even if it means they'll possibly be promoted into new positions outside your department. When you champion your staff members, they'll pay you back through dedication, respect, and hard work.

Our Teams

~ 15 ~

Competition versus Cooperation

For long-term success, avoid unhealthy competition and reward your employees for cooperation and teamwork.

Josee and her Great Dane friend, Timothy, love playing tug. One Thanksgiving Friday, Timothy's owner, Mitchell, dropped his dog off before going out of town for the holiday weekend. The two old buddies were ecstatic to be together—especially since Timothy had brought along his stuffed pink piglet. Being such a gentle giant, Timothy has toys to match, so this toy was the size of a real piglet.

True to form, the play began as soon as Josee and Timothy set eyes on each other. And the poor, unsuspecting stuffed piglet was pulled in most directions of the compass as the two dogs tussled over it. With Josee and Timothy, tug is an endurance test. Either of them will initiate the game in their own personality style: Timothy will subtly pick up a toy and walk past Josee with the object in his mouth, dangling it near her face. Josee, as always, is more direct, so she simply grabs a toy, usually from Timothy's collection, and then runs over to him and pushes it towards his mouth. They play tug for long periods of time, fully engaged. It's best to keep out of the way while they're doing this, since you may be bumped off your feet if you get too close. When the tugging went on too long that weekend, I separated them—Josee going

103

to her favourite chair and Timothy to his bed—so I could enjoy some peace and quiet.

On Saturday morning, Mark and I were enjoying a peaceful cup of coffee in the living room when the dogs decided to play yet another game of tug. Timothy, well rested from a good night's sleep, wandered over to his bed and picked up his piglet. Sauntering around the room as if he had no particular plans in mind, he passed Josee as slowly as he could, and Josee took the bait, grabbing the butt end of the piglet with lightning speed.

The game was on! They tugged away as if their lives depended upon getting that piglet away from the opposite side. We could hear growling, and the action was incredible as their paws were scraped along the carpet. All of a sudden, the noise stopped, and we saw, to our surprise, that Timothy was holding the piglet so Josee could get a better grip on it. As play resumed, there were more growls and panting, followed only a few moments later by another quiet spell as Josee held the toy so *Timothy* could get a better hold on it. Mark and I just sat there, enjoying our front-row seats as this pattern of cooperative play continued. We noticed that those pauses were not just isolated events; they made up a central feature of their mutual play. Their goal was to have the most fun possible by making sure both of them won. They didn't actually care which dog got the piglet in the end.

By Monday morning, that poor little piglet had become the sacrificial Thanksgiving pig. They'd had the best time possible with that stuffed toy because neither of them was trying to win. They just wanted to keep on playing together. A game like tug-of-war suggests that one team or player is the victor, while the other is defeated entirely. The two playing pups changed this into a mutual game, where the dog with the weakest hold at a particular moment was given help by the other. They realized that to continue to play together effectively, they both needed to have a good, firm hold on the toy at all times.

How does your team operate? Do your team members help each other out when they're losing their grip on what they need to accomplish? Or does one person or a select group try to take power and outshine the others? Is your team built on values of competition or cooperation? Traditionally, business has been based on competition, but this can be counterproductive. Do you have charts that log bonuses for people who sell or produce more than others? This type of approach creates a competition, and competition creates a win-lose scenario, where one person is the top dog, others take second place, and someone is always at the bottom of the heap. Winning can bring great feelings of success, but losing can be demotivating. Rather than creating a supportive team, competition can break a team into factions as people attempt to outdo each other.

At one Canadian service-based company, management set up a system to evaluate the success of their service teams. They ran a contest between regions based on key technician performance indicators, such as appointment arrival times, first-time-right installations, and repeat service calls. The intent was to improve customer relations. The contest was a horse race. Every week, the service team in each area was evaluated and given points based on the team's weekly results. The group that rated number 1 in each region was awarded 4 points; the last team was given 0 points for the week. The area that crossed the finish line first was the big winner.

The winning team was promoted within the company as number 1 in communications bulletins and at meetings. Unfortunately, this system pitted one team against the other. As a result of the rivalry, many managers were secretive about best practices for success, holding back information that would have benefited the whole company. For example, when the Northern Regional Manager asked the Central Regional Manager what they were doing, he would say, "Nothing really, just coaching our technicians."

By contrast, Joanne, the Ontario Regional Manager, was extremely successful with her statistics, including installations, service calls, and preventing repeat service calls. One manager contacted Joanne to find out what she was doing to create such success in her team. She freely shared her team's area report, which included their successes and their challenges. These were the processes that her team found most helpful:

- reminding technicians about the fundamentals by putting them back through basic training
- having struggling technicians job-shadow those who were successful
- sending field managers out to other regions to job-shadow and observe best practices
- seeking feedback from the field to discover what tools and equipment the technicians needed to do a better job

As a result of her collaborative management style within her team and with the other regional managers, metrics increased throughout all regions, and the company as a whole had better bottom-line results.

Bringing this back to the team level, can you afford to pit individual against individual within your team? Is this the message you want to send? How might you send a message indicating that joint effort is the most highly valued approach in your department? In teams where more value is placed on competition than on collaboration, the resulting dynamics are damaging to the team as a whole.

The table below identifies the common differences between competitive (non-trusting) and collaborative (trusting) team dynamics.

Type of Team	Competitive Team (like the one in the Northern Region)	Collaborative Team (like the one in the Ontario Region)
Typical Dynamics	Individual is the priority	Team is the priority
	Withholding information that may be critical to team success	Sharing information, data, and ideas to ensure team success

Type of Team	Competitive Team (like the one in the Northern Region)	Collaborative Team (like the one in the Ontario Region)
Typical Dynamics	Back-stabbing behaviour, attempts to consciously sabotage others' efforts (e.g., information hoarding)	Cooperative behaviour (e.g., helping when another team member is extremely busy)
	Moving into cliques that have similar perspectives	Being inclusive of all team members and supporting ideas, even when differences arise
	Lack of trust	Trust, confidence that team support will always be there
	Defensiveness, arguing	Openness and cooperation
	Conflict	Harmony
	Increased team challenges, creating difficulty in achieving success	Increased team unity and success

When competitive behaviours occur in teams, the result can be lack of trust, leading to fragmentation within the team. In a scenario where a prize or bonus is offered to the top producer or seller, individuals will not only strive to reach the top at the expense of team building; they may also undermine each other to get the prize. After all, there is only one prize to win, and people love to win prizes. The problem is that in this win-lose scenario, the consistent loser is teamwork.

Competitions like this are also based on the assumption that each team member should have the same strengths and abilities. Such a simplistic challenge to motivate a team can do the very opposite. Individuals who believe internally that they don't have the skills to win the contest may think, "Why spend energy doing something I can't do very well?" As a result, they may be demotivated. This type of "motivation" puts undue stress on the individuals who are less proficient.

When teams operate as Josee and Timothy did—in a spirit of collaboration and cooperation—they experience a sense of camaraderie. Knowing that a team member will "hold the toy" for you when you are struggling is priceless. After all, solid team work is based on supporting and helping one another achieve the best outcomes. If you decide to have a contest in your workplace, ensure that prizes are awarded fairly—not to just one individual who consistently outproduces the others. Set up a fair competition that makes teamwork a priority and where recognition will be given when team members work together and help each other achieve the best outcomes. This will enable all team members to use their personal strengths to reach the goals as a team.

If a corporate competition is launched, check with your manager to discuss how you can nurture teamwork within the overall contest. Ask for funds to be added to, or reallocated to, your employee recognition budget, to ensure that you can reward your employees for teamwork, not just achievement, when they reach the finish line. If you are unsuccessful in having the money redistributed within your budget, invite your team to think of creative ways to participate in the contest while remaining collaborative in their work.

For instance, each employee could submit the names of people who helped them with tasks they could not perform so well themselves or perhaps, as a team, they could submit one person's name into the company contest and then share the prize, all the time knowing that they all won.

Remember to lead by example. If you exhibit competition with other managers, you are modelling competitive behaviour. Making an off-the-cuff negative comment that puts down another manager can do more damage to your team than you might expect—like a spoiled apple that ruins the entire bushel. Once you utter the words, even in frustration, your level of integrity and respect will go down. People may wonder what you are saying about *them* behind their backs, and this, in turn, creates fear and mistrust of you as a manager.

Make a commitment to yourself and to your team never to make any negative comments or spread any gossip about another employee—whether that person is part of your own team or part of your management team. Instead, practise mentorship by offering supportive and constructive feedback directly to individuals and teams.

Remember the power of the win-win scenario. Avoid the win-lose scenario at all costs. Before endorsing a contest, ask yourself the following questions:

- How might my team collaborate to meet the goal so everyone wins?
- In what other ways might I keep all team members motivated and focused on the goal?
- How might I engage all skill sets equally, in order to achieve positive outcomes?
- How might I reduce tension and increase cross-function support?
- In what different ways might the goal be achieved in order to ensure the active involvement of all employees?
- What rewards can I offer that will motivate my employees to make contributions to the team effort?

Be like Joanne and share information that will lead to the company's overall success, rather than getting caught up in winning the prize. Ensure that you recognize and acknowledge team cooperation and collaboration throughout the entire process—not when the goal has been reached.

If you use this approach, your team, like Josee and Timothy, will have more fun, they'll reach their goals more easily, and they'll bond in ways that will create a team spirit to carry them through many future achievements and challenges!

~ 16 ~

Using the Resources on Your Team

*Every employee has innate skills and abilities
that can benefit your team.*

Josee loves water. As part Labrador Retriever, bred for finding ducks and other prey in lakes and oceans, she is naturally drawn to the stuff. Even before she knew she could swim, she would love to roll in, run into, and splash in water. And she's expert at sniffing out the H_2O. No matter how small a stream, ditch, or swamp might be, she'll run through forests, under fences, and into long grass to find it. She's such an expert at this that I've nicknamed her "Water Witch."

One sunny fall afternoon, we went out to the country to a popular dog-walking site, Starkey's Hill. It's actually a combination of hills and valleys—great for hiking—and that day, the leaves were turning gorgeous shades of crimson and orange and falling gently all around us. We were having a family walk, Josee, Mark, and I. Our only priority that day was to get some exercise and enjoy the outdoors. Time was no object.

Then ... as we came up over a hill, enjoying the scents of the dying leaves, we were assaulted by something that didn't smell good at all. We watched powerlessly from the top of the rise as Josee, true to form, proceeded to run full speed into the swamp for a swim. She came out when we went down and called her, happily running around us, shaking off the water and liberally distributing the swampy smells. Our cute little dog had changed into a swamp monster. Since my husband and I are city dwellers who don't like our dog to stink, we drove directly to the local dog-washing station to clean her up.

Most of the time, though, my husband and I love to let Josee swim. It's great exercise for her, and paddling and playing in water is one of her innate skills. She would be unhappy and unfulfilled if she didn't go on her water-searching missions, and we would miss out on the joy of watching her splash around.

Do you want your team members to use their natural abilities and expertise at work? Absolutely. Everyone has unique aptitudes that enable them to work in a way that creates meaning for them, and this, in turn, produces good results for the team. By identifying your staff's innate talents, you'll be able to motivate them by letting them use their passions and expertise. You can encourage these folks to be themselves as long as they are not making a "stink." This will allow team members to seek out resources and generate innovative solutions to challenges. Having workers who, like Josee, are highly motivated—in fact, impassioned—by their goals is a gift. When left to their own devices, these individuals will work diligently until they succeed.

To determine each person's work style, simply ask them:

- What is your favourite part of your job?
- When do you feel most in your "zone"?
- What tasks do you find easiest to complete?
- What makes you leave work with a sense of satisfaction?
- What expertise do you bring to our team?

It can also be helpful to observe your staff to get a better understanding of their work preferences. Who is great at dealing with crises and deadlines? Who takes longer to discuss ideas in a team meeting because they are more skilled than others at viewing a project from multiple perspectives? Who plays the devil's advocate, presenting reservations about proposed ideas? Perhaps their innate skill is to uncover a potential problem so it can be resolved before a project begins. Some employees may need to chat or even vent with others to assimilate the next steps of their work. Others may simply need to be left alone to focus. If you're aware of skills like these, you'll be able to assign work based on your team members' preferences. You'll also know when they're out of their comfort zones, and you'll then be able to check in with them to find out whether they need extra support.

I know an experienced group therapist who was working in a program with a number of other skilled counsellors. They each had their own unique style of group facilitation that fit for them and created great results for their clients. Then their supervisor decided to standardize the treatment that all clients received. The result was high stress and low morale among the facilitators. Though the supervisor had some good reasons for introducing the standardization, the program became less effective for the clients, since the facilitators were unable to use their innate skills and individual techniques.

To ensure that your employees feel respected for their skills, make sure that your company's goals, values and objectives are understood. Help people understand the policy frameworks that are not negotiable. It's best to do this when individuals first begin working in your department or shortly after you accept your position as supervisor or manager. Then, to make sure that you don't suppress helpful skills among your staff, hold a team meeting where all members will have the opportunity to tell you what they need to work effectively. Then, with your guidance, have the team members themselves set some of the norms of their workplace. This will help them become more engaged in respecting all the norms governing your department.

It can also be helpful to have your staff review department policies on a yearly basis—perhaps at the same time as their performance appraisal. When the team is clear and has some input into department goals and rules for behaviour ahead of time, they will be more likely to buy into them. This will make it easier for you to deal with shortfalls or inappropriate behaviour when they arise.

From a team perspective, it's best to let your team members find or create their own working styles as long as those methods are moral and legal. Trust your employees to create the schedules and discipline they need to complete their projects successfully. Make sure that you respect their work styles even if you'd prefer to have them use different methods. When you expend energy to prevent your staff from working in their own style, you give the message that they are lacking and somehow unacceptable. Many employees will simply nod and give you lip service but then go right back to carrying out their tasks in their own way. Worse, your employees may become demotivated by such a critique or at the very least become frustrated with you.

When your employees are committed to the team's objectives and are taking action towards a common outcome, it's best to allow personal work styles to flourish. If Josee was always prevented from finding water, she would simply become more creative and work harder to get the swimming and splashing exercise she wants. Training her to avoid water would be time consuming and difficult, and in the process, she would lose a part of who she is.

As manager or supervisor, be crystal clear about your goals, expectations, and timelines for each specific project. But then give your team members the space to shine within their own processes and work styles. When you get out of their way and respect their individual styles, you'll find that they'll work harder, they'll be more engaged, and they'll get the job done faster and with less effort.

There may well be times when a particular employee's work style prevents them from reaching team objectives. In cases like this, you'll need to address the problem. Help this team member discover what they need to change in order to meet deadlines and expectations. Ask them where they're having difficulty. Help them review what's working for them and support them as they make changes that will enhance their natural style. Guide them into success by suggesting a few adjustments to improve their work habits. Then check back with them to see how the modifications are working.

If you discover that any of your workers are delving into the world of immoral or illegal behaviour, deal with the problem quickly and directly. Take a moment to record your observations about the situation, including the date, time, and location of the incident and how you became aware of it. This will help you have more clarity when meeting with Human Resources and your manager. It will be imperative to contact the Human Resources Department and your manager to determine the best steps to take in your organization.

Allowing your employees to work in the manner that is most effective for them within the bounds of appropriate behaviour will enable them to be more productive. Don't waste your valuable time fighting something that works for another person. You may even learn a few methods that you'll want to add to your own work repertoire.

Mark and I will never be swimmers like Josee, but if we didn't give her the freedom to enjoy that innate talent, we'd all miss out on many hours of joy. Similarly, giving your employees reasonable latitude in applying their natural gifts will bring pleasure and productivity to your workplace.

~ 17 ~

Loyalty

Loyalty is a two-way street.
Treating employees with acceptance and trust will encourage
them to trust you. The result? A solid pillar of loyalty.

My friend Sophia is a dog person who is now retired after years of working in the animal health field. She's a calm, thoughtful person and an amazing listener who gives great feedback based on her insights. She has two dogs, Ben and Mickey, who are at either end of the age spectrum. Ben is a 15-year-old black-and-white mixed breed with spots on his legs, and Mickey is a black Lab. Ben has some mobility issues, so he has trouble getting into the back seat of the car, and he no longer takes the stairs to bed at night. He also suffers from limited vision and hearing, and all of these things make him a little grumpy at times. Mickey is a three-year-old bull in the china shop. When her 74 pounds of pure puppy exuberance run into you, you feel as if you've been struck by an ocean freighter.

One sunny March afternoon, Josee and I invited Sophia, Ben, and Mickey to join us for a walk. The temperatures that day were slightly above average, and there was a small breeze. It felt like freedom to go outside wearing a light jacket instead of a big parka. We met at the entrance to an old gravel pit trail. This vast open space covers acres of land but has only a scattering of trees and a small creek running through the centre—nothing of great visual beauty. You might wonder why anyone would walk their dog there. Well, it's an amazing place for dogs even though it's not a human paradise. And walking around in that old pit helps calm me at a deep level, as I can stroll at a leisurely pace, knowing Josee is safe (because there are no roads for her to run onto).

For Josee, the old gravel area is a place to run freely, play with other dogs, and swim in the creek. And in the spring, she splashes around in puddles that young kids have dug to make obstacle courses for their bikes. These puddles fill up and turn the lovely hue of chocolate milk. Fortunately, the swimming hole has clean, fresh water, and it's closer to the exit, so Josee goes there for a clean-up swim after getting covered with the chocolate mud.

That day in March, Sophia was thrilled to come along, since Mickey and Josee could play in their usual exuberant way while Ben could amble along at his older-dog pace. True to form, Ben wandered off alone to sniff around, and Josee and Mickey charged off together as Sophia and I strolled along the mucky, muddy path in our rubber boots. All was going according to plan.

But every so often, Mickey would run straight towards Ben and plough right into him. Sophia would cringe whenever she saw poor Ben enduring this mistreatment from his younger sister, but the older dog simply stood his ground, allowing Mickey to be herself, tolerating her behaviour. Josee would run around the two of them in her own joyful way, enjoying what she thought was a delightful game.

About halfway through our 45-minute walk, as Sophia and I rounded a corner, we realized that Ben was no longer in our sight lines. Mickey, who had gone on ahead of us with Josee, suddenly stopped running and turned around, clearly looking to see where Ben had gone. Sophia encouraged Mickey to keep running ahead of us, but Mickey would not move. It was as if she'd lost part of her team and was searching for it ... She stood still and kept looking around until she finally saw her beloved old Ben. Then, at warp speed, she ran towards him and ran circles around him. Josee followed suit.

Sophia and I started chatting about how loyal Mickey is to Ben. Despite having another youthful playmate, she needed to be sure that Ben was okay and was still part of the team. Ben had had Sophia and the house to himself until the ripe old age of 12, when Mickey came to live with them. And even though he can be grumpy at times, he always tolerates Mickey's behaviour and never snaps at her. As a result, Ben is rewarded with pure and unwavering loyalty from the young black Lab.

Managers and supervisors also need to develop loyalty on their teams. When employees are loyal, an environment of respect, cooperation, and dedication to the team's goals can be nurtured. But how do you create a loyal employee? Do you know what your employees truly want? What key principles do you need to adhere to so employees will be motivated to stay with your department or company over the long term?

First, let's review what all employees truly want from an employer. Generally, they want a few simple things: to feel respected, to be honoured for their contribution to the team, and to be treated well through departmental and company policies and procedures. When someone new joins the team, you, as supervisor or manager, have a great opportunity to respond to them in ways that will encourage them to stay with you for a long time. Many newcomers are full of enthusiasm and can even be a bit "over the top"—like Mickey. In cases like this, do you act like Ben and tolerate their sometimes overly exuberant behaviour or do you become overwhelmed and try to stifle them?

As a supervisor or manager, it's vital to learn ways to not just tolerate, but also appreciate the excitement of someone who's new to the job. While new employees may be a bit "clumsy," like Mickey, they are often highly motivated, and if you support this energy and help the new person channel it in a productive way, you may find yourself at the beginning of a long relationship of dedication to your team. Youthful exuberance can also go a long way to revitalizing the existing team. So be sure to listen fully to the new employee's input and show interest in their fresh ideas, which are not influenced by years of working in the same environment. If, at the same time, you help your new team member acclimatize to the team's culture, you'll bring benefits to the entire team as well as to your recently hired employee.

It's always best practice to ensure that you listen fully to input from all employees. Sometimes, what appears to be the craziest idea going is the beginning of an amazing solution to a chronic problem. Let your team member know that you're listening fully to their ideas by reflecting back to them the information they shared with you. When an idea is viable, take steps to implement it in some form. This will show the employee that they've been heard, that they've been honoured for their contribution to the team, that they have influence within the workplace. When employees know that they can have an impact on their work environment, they experience a sense of empowerment, and this, in turn, creates fully engaged employees who become loyal. Another way to help staff feel valued is to make certain that the policies and procedures of the department recognize employees for their dedication and hard work. If policies and procedures don't reflect these values, then alter them where possible.

One employer operated from one-sided policies that favoured the agency all the time. For example, once a week, therapists on staff were scheduled to work a 12-hour day, dealing with abused clients. The interactions were demanding, as the therapists were dealing with intense emotions, crises, and problematic behaviour. While the work itself was rewarding, employees felt no loyalty due to the company's employer-first policies. So once the work of the day was done, staff often left a few minutes early—partly because of exhaustion and partly because they had to be back at work first thing in the morning, ready to work with the same high-needs clients.

One member of the team was taking karate lessons and, at one point, he told the supervisor about them. During the course of that conversation, the supervisor realized that the employee was leaving early, and the employee, trying to get himself out of hot water, said that others commonly left 10 minutes early.

Rather than appreciating that the staff were all working like dogs, that they were exhausted, and that they needed to be back in 11 hours to work their next shift, the supervisor reprimanded all members of the team. In fact, he told his staff, "You're stealing from the agency by leaving early. You must all remain in your offices until 9:00 p.m." He'd forgotten that only a few years earlier, when he'd been in the same position as his staff, he'd also left early. From then on, the therapists did all stay until their shifts were officially over, but they resented the fact that their supervisor didn't recognize their extremely hard work and didn't trust them to keep on putting in a full day's work in spite of leaving just a few minutes early.

The employee who was taking karate lessons once had a client who was feeling suicidal. He took the client to the hospital and spent two hours supporting the client. When he asked for time off in lieu of the two hours of overtime incurred, his request was rejected, since he hadn't had his time preapproved.

As a result of these two decisions, the employee realized that his efforts were not respected and that he was not a valued employee, so he was no longer motivated to go above and beyond for his employer as he had in the past.

Unfortunately, his fellow employees all felt the same, and they all eventually left this workplace. When a supervisor or manager fails to recognize the extra effort of even one employee, other team members will notice, and then everyone on the team will lose motivation to go the extra mile. If this lack of appreciation extends to many or all team members, loyalty will vanish and so will the employees.

Of course, policies and procedures are created to be followed, but it's important not to be too rigid about them. When your staff is diligent and is meeting deadlines or getting their work done early and when they're producing quality results, it might be appropriate to allow them to leave early to attend a doctor's appointment or to deal with family issues. You could even make it a habit to let your employees leave early on Fridays. As you listen to input from your team members, implement their ideas, and administer policies in a manner that produces a win-win situation, you will be making goodwill deposits that will build up over time.

How will this technique help you and your department? Once your employees experience this goodwill, they'll be more likely to develop loyalty to you and the company. Then they'll want to make you shine in the eyes of your boss, and they'll be dedicated to ensuring that work is done on time and to the best of their ability.

Research has shown that employees do not feel valued because of their wages alone. Many employers feel that they can offer good pay and then relax. They don't think of offering any other reward or recognition for employee contributions. Wrong! In fact, being respected, being acknowledged, and having good benefits are higher priorities for employees. Remember the Platinum Rule: treat others as they want to be treated. Don't be like the supervisor in the example described above, who developed amnesia about what it's like to work in the trenches. Think about your employees' day-to-day lives in the workplace and about their ongoing contributions to the success of your department.

- What are their greatest challenges?
- What parts of their jobs are annoying for them?
- If you were doing their jobs, what would you want in terms of respect, response to suggestions, and policies?

- How can you deliver what they truly need to do their jobs better?
- How can you be flexible with department policies to ensure that employees feel valued?
- Do you have a solid benefits package even for your part-time employees?

If not, what steps might you take to investigate the costs and advocate on their behalf for better benefits? If your employees don't have the added worry of what happens if they get ill or how they'll cover the costs of dental work, eyeglasses, and medications, they'll be much more likely to stay with your organization longer, and they'll have more energy to focus on their work.

In short, help your employees feel that they're valued members of the "family" by respecting their input, listening fully to their ideas for improvement by implementing them when possible, and remembering to treat them as they want to be treated! Give them the security of the best benefits package that you can afford. You'll reap the benefits of your goodwill deposits with interest in the form of having employees who are dedicated to you and their work.

So be like Ben who was flexible enough to accept Mickey's behaviour as long as it didn't get out of hand. He was rewarded by loyalty, and you will be too.

~ 18 ~

Shadows: Overcoming Distractions

*Learning to overcome distractions will create
a more satisfying work experience.*

It was a morning of intermittent sunshine, so I'd turned on the ceiling-fan lights in the living room, where I was working away on my laptop. But then the sun started shining intensely through our dining room windows and into the living room. It created a comfy atmosphere, but it also threw a glare on my computer screen, which distracted me from the words I was typing.

Then I noticed something out of the corner of my eye: it was Josee, standing in front of her favourite, green-leather chair as if she was asking permission to jump up and sit on it. Instead of clambering onto her sleeping spot the way she usually does, she kept looking at the chair and then at me. So, distracted from my work again, I glanced over at the chair and noticed that Mark had left a blanket and the TV remote on it when he'd gone to bed the night before. I got up and removed the inconvenient objects, and Josee promptly jumped up and rolled into a ball and was soon in slumberland.

I returned to the couch to resume my writing. Then it was full steam ahead with complete concentration until Josee woke up and jumped down from her perch. I could see, out of the corner of my eye, that she was doing something unusual, so I set my laptop down and watched her. The intensity of the sunlight and the light in the ceiling fan had combined to make Josee's shadow quite dark, and she was playing with it as if it were a real object or another dog. Holding in my laughter to make sure I didn't disrupt her playing, I watched her in amazement as she frolicked with her shadow self.

Josee has a habit of rubbing the sides of her neck on things. She generally uses this technique only when we're hiking in nature, and then she often rubs her neck in something disgusting that smells. I've been told that dogs do this to cover up their own scent when hunting, to make sure their potential prey won't smell them coming. But this morning in our living room, I noticed that Josee was rolling in her shadow in a similar way. I kept watching in awe as she continued to play-wrestle with her silhouette.

At times, Josee would look away and pretend she didn't see it, so she could launch a surprise attack on it. She played in this way for several minutes, still trying to catch her shadow, though it would always disappear as she got close. Then she got an itch and stopped to scratch. As she raised her back paw to do the scratching, she was distracted by that darned shadow, which had moved! She forgot about the itch and started playing with the mysterious shape again.

I thought about how common it is for people at work to become distracted from the task at hand, just like me being distracted by Josee and Josee forgetting about her itch to chase that shadow. These days, it's very easy to get sidetracked from our work, even at the office. We're inundated by multiple daily tasks and long-term demands and also have voicemail and email interruptions to deal with.

Here's how it often goes. You begin your day with the best of intentions. You're highly motivated, and you've decided to stay focused today. You get to your desk, and as you're booting up your computer, you take a few moments to listen to your voicemail messages. Writing down the messages, you realize that three new priorities have been added to your list of things to do. Then you remind yourself that you're going to be so productive today. You sign onto your computer and check your emails—which bring forward a number of quick tasks that people want you to do. You decide to take a few moments to respond to their requests. After all, they're small items and won't take much time. You look at your clock and realize it's almost lunchtime. You groan in frustration, realizing that you've become distracted after all and your productive day is almost half over. You've spent your morning in reaction mode, responding to the priorities of other people.

There are so many "bright, shiny objects" that can take an employee off focus—voicemail, email, Web browsing, and social media, to name a few. When you look up something on the Internet and you see a link to something else that interests you, it's so easy to think, "I'll just take a second and look at that one." After you've checked it out, you realize that half an hour has passed, and you have to make an effort to pull yourself away from that website and get back to your work.

How many times do your team members get caught in the shadow of social media? How many times do they take a few moments to post an update on Facebook and then see something else that interests them? Taking a few moments to check out that item results in lost work time. While the actual sidetrack might absorb only a few minutes, the human mind takes about 20 minutes to regain concentration on another task. From this perspective, these little distractions can become very expensive because of the downtime they take away from the day, and this, in turn, reduces productivity in the workplace.

How do you shift from distraction and reaction into productive mode? As an employee, you can do a number of things to reduce the risk of losing time. First, be clear about the tasks required on a given day, to make sure you have a focus for that day. Write a to-do list at the end of each day for the following day and then cross off each item as it is completed. Check your voicemail and email when you are between specific tasks instead of every 5 to 15 minutes. I attended a productivity workshop a few years ago where the speaker suggested that we start our days by working on tasks from our to-do lists and check our emails later in the morning. If you start out by checking your emails, someone else's priorities or crisis will take over the agenda for that day, and your own priorities will suffer, only to be done later on, under greater pressure.

In our culture, where we've come to expect instantaneous communications, we've lost touch with what a crisis truly is. We get news immediately from across the globe, and we think we'll miss a vital message if we don't check our emails every 15 minutes. We respond right away, as if there truly was a crisis, and this causes a stressed interruption, because our brains are constantly trying to focus on a variety of tasks at the same time.

It can be helpful to set an alarm for 40 minutes and dedicate that amount of time to a specific project. Once the alarm goes off, take the time to check your voicemail and emails. Then take 10 minutes to refocus on your priorities for the next 40-minute period and set the alarm again. By dividing your day into 40-minute intervals, your brain will be able to focus on the task at hand. After your second 40-minute period, it will probably be time to take a break and refresh yourself. You may find that 40-minute periods don't work well for you. In that case, try 35- or 50-minute intervals—or a time period in this range that will help you become uber productive.

Stanley, a bank loans officer, would spend hours of his time playing games on his computer, paying personal bills, and not focusing on his work at all. One of his co-workers, who had to go to reception frequently to receive clients, began to notice his activities. Each time she passed by Stanley's office, he was on the phone on a personal call (the co-worker could tell by the dialogue) or playing games on his computer. He was supposed to be catching up on paperwork, but none of that was happening. A worker like Stanley would need to be dealt with individually and have his work performance addressed.

As a supervisor or manager, how do you help your team members deal with potential distractions? Do you require them to check their emails as soon as they arrive at work? Is there room for flexibility in this expectation? Would crises really happen if they waited until 40 minutes into their workday before checking their emails for the first time? As a team, have a discussion about checking emails and determine the best way to manage this task. Brainstorm ideas that others could apply to their working days to help them remain focused.

If you have an employee who is struggling to get through their workload, ask them how they deal with email, voicemail, and Web browsing. Ask them what they need to focus on most. Have the employee set up a plan of action that will focus their day more effectively, and give them feedback on it. Let them know that you're there as a resource to help with their plan, but let the team member come up with their own suggestions. Perhaps they need to close their email for periods during the day, or at the very least, remove email notifications from their screen. If the noise of individuals in nearby cubicles distracts them, it may be helpful to let employees listen to low-volume music on a device that has earbuds. You could also install a white-noise sound machine.

When a team member is chronically late for deadlines, it is good practice to inquire about how they manage their day. Ask what causes distractions for them. It may be noise from nearby co-workers; a personal crisis at home; or the conflicting demands of email, voicemail, and websites. Ask the employee what would help them focus better. Find out whether they're using a to-do list. Is the to-do list in an electronic file near their email inbox? If it is, ask whether they get sidetracked by emails when looking at their schedule? Can they create a list in another program or use the old-fashioned pen-and-paper method?

Review the methods your employee uses to prioritize their emails. Do they use subfolders to organize the emails? Do they flag priorities and reduce the number of emails in their inbox to a minimum to prevent having to needlessly search through unrelated messages to find the one they need to respond to? Help them organize their emails and to-do list in a way that fits for them. It's important not to impose a particular organizational system on your employee. We all need to organize ourselves in a way that works for us. Ask your team member to keep track of the amount of time they spend on email, social media, and websites. It may be helpful to suggest that they check email and social media only at specific times during the day and that they track the amount of time they spend being distracted by websites they don't need to consult.

Everyone gets distracted from time to time. The challenge is to minimize distractions so employees can be as productive as possible. And working at high efficiency will enable your team members to leave at the end of each day with a sense of accomplishment, knowing that they crossed plenty of items off their to-do lists.

Learning our own personal styles for minimizing interruptions will lower stress levels and increase productivity. Find out what your shadows are and think of creative ways to stop paying too much attention to them. Then you'll feel good about the amount you've accomplished by the end of the day.

~ 19 ~

Pylons Gone Bad: Fun and Work

Allowing laughter and play in the team
reduces stress and increases creativity.

When Josee was a small puppy, we'd go to a park where she could run and play in the open grass, on the baseball diamond, and in the football field. We'd arrive in the early morning when no sports teams were around, so she had plenty of space to roam. She'd run at top speed around the park, blowing off steam and smiling from ear to ear—or would that be from jowl to jowl?

One day when we arrived at the park for her early morning play, she discovered a small orange pylon. It was only about five inches tall, but she was mesmerized by it. She ran over to it immediately, grabbed it in her little mouth, and ran around joyously with her "prize." I found myself smiling and laughing as I experienced her pleasure, focusing only on how incredibly cute and happy she was.

A few weeks later, we arrived at the park at mid-morning and found that the football field had been taken over by a high school football team. So I took Josee to the opposite end of the park near the baseball diamond to make sure we didn't interrupt their practice. As we walked by, I observed the team, dressed in full pads. Some of the guys who were standing around appeared to be bored by the drills. Then Josee ran right into the field, and my efforts to keep her away from the team turned out to be in vain.

It took me only a few seconds to realize why Josee had charged into the field. The coach had set up a whole lot of those lovely little pylons for the team to run through as part of their drills. I watched powerlessly as, within seconds, Josee sprinted down the field—touchdown! She grabbed a pylon from the field, took it in her mouth, and with pride and delight, proceeded to run and bounce all through the football practice.

When Josee is playful and happy, which, frankly, is most of the time, her delight is infectious. The young men on the football team thought her routines were hilarious. In fact, all members of the team formed a huddle around Josee, laughing, joking, petting her, and generally having a great time. As this was all happening, I looked over at the coach. He didn't seem to be so impressed by the interference. But he did smile a few times and was probably wondering if he was ever going to get the team to meet his objectives that morning.

I called Josee away from the spellbound young men, but at that time, her recall skills (that is, coming when I called her) were weak at best. When she was engaged with something she was enjoying, she would be so entrenched in her activity that I did not exist in her mind. I ended up calling over to one of the guys to grab her by the collar, which he happily did. I sheepishly went and got her, apologizing profusely to the coach. I put Josee on her leash and promptly got her out of the park.

As we walked away, I looked back at the team and the coach to see their reactions. The guys were still laughing, while the coach, not surprisingly, appeared to be slightly exasperated. I was curious about what he would do next, so I kept watching. Clearly, he had a choice to make—either let his frustration show and take it out on the team or roll with it and get back to the practice.

The coach handled the situation like a pro. "Okay, guys," he said, "let's get back to doing the drills." He tolerated their fun, allowed them to embrace it, and then made the call to get back to work. Soon, the practice was back in session and the young men were now fully engaged, taking the spirit of excitement with them into practising their drills. In fact, the guys appeared to have shifted from being barely interested in their practice to being fully immersed in the drills and enjoying the work. My guess is that Josee was a minor celebrity in their school that day as the football players recounted the story.

What happens in your workplace when team members are taking a break from their routines and having fun? How do you deal with this as a supervisor or manager? Do you allow your team members to enjoy themselves or do you try to pull them out of the experience and rush them back to work? Do you join in the fun?

It's important to remember that teams who laugh together also work well together. Humour in the workplace can have numerous benefits, including relieving boredom, enhancing team cohesiveness, and relieving stress. Recognize that your staff is often under the pressure of multiple deadlines and expectations and that laughter can help them reduce stress and re-engage in their work. Laughing will also increase the amount of oxygen in their systems, and this will actually make them think more clearly. The endorphins released when people laugh enhance brain function by increasing the activity of neurotransmitters in the brain, and this results in a better mood, a greater sense of well-being, and more creativity. All of these things will improve problem solving and will therefore result in a more productive work environment. Allow yourself to relax and enjoy the fun too. You'll be rejuvenated, and so will your employees.

In teams where the supervisor or manager stifles the fun, employees tend to experience increased stress and may develop a "walking on eggshells" approach to the work environment. In a context like this, team members will always be "looking over their shoulders" and feeling on guard in relation to management. When employees experience their fun being stifled, they tend to be more cautious in their work environment. The fear of getting caught enjoying themselves may result in more play and play that is less appropriate. For instance, your staff may start having fun at someone else's expense. It may be you, the manager, who the team experiences as a killjoy.

There's a natural rhythm to interactions on teams, where employees go from being fully engaged in their work to having fun times to just taking breaks to relax together. Accepting this natural ebb and flow will enable your team to be more successful.

Workers who are employed in these accepting workplaces tend to experience a sense of confidence in one another and greater camaraderie. This will help them manoeuvre through high-stress periods. Team members will begin to recognize that by playing together, working together becomes easier and more satisfying. When we take pleasure in our work, we are more likely to be fully engrossed in it. And when employees know that management wants them to have some fun, they're likely to have a greater sense of empowerment because they will realize that their managers respect them. As a result, your employees will work hard, play hard, and find creative ways to reach team targets.

Back on the football field, where Josee was distracting everyone from their practice, I imagine the coach was also enjoying the moment and saw Josee's antics as a bit funny as well. He stayed calm and allowed for a few moments of distraction and then gently and firmly brought the team back together. That way, the team had some fun and resumed practice in a more engaged manner.

Perhaps, if the coach was reading this chapter now, he might wonder what would have happened if he had allowed himself to laugh with the players. Would the team have bonded with him even more? Would they have tried harder to please him, knowing that he had their backs?

When your team is enjoying an amusing moment, do you worry that they won't get back on track? Do you feel left out? How do you react—by interrupting the merriment? Or do you act like the coach and tolerate it? Have you considered engaging with your team by laughing and playing with them? I propose that by taking part in your employees' enjoyment, they'll feel more secure with you. They can engage in fun, get the job done and know that as a manager, you honour their process.

If you're struggling to accept your team having fun, sit back and remind yourself about the last time this happened.

- Did the time out help the team meet their deadline or did it hinder them?
- How did the laughter help the work process?
- After they'd had a good laugh, were your employees more creative or inventive in their solutions?
- Did the fun times help relieve a stressful environment?
- Were your employees laughing at anyone else's expense?
- Was the fun offensive to anyone?
- Did the team return to work shortly afterwards and with more energy?

If the play had any negative components, you will need to address this. Set a boundary with the individual team members who were involved. If there were no setbacks, remind yourself that having fun is a natural and important aspect of team interaction. Know that you can trust the professionalism of your team enough that you can let them play. Work and play go hand in hand, and both are needed to create a successful workplace.

So next time your team is having some frivolous fun, sit back, watch them interact, and perhaps even engage. Laugh along and enjoy the greater respect they will have for you. You may also experience the side effects that I do with Josee. As I watch her joyfully engaged in play, all I feel is pleasure and renewal in my heart, and my stress seems to melt away.

Check your budget and set up some fun opportunities for your team. What about doing an improv workshop? That can be an excellent team-enhancing experience. What about going bowling for an afternoon? Or letting the team create an experience that they would enjoy that also fits your budget. If you don't have the financial resources to do this, you could consider holding a half-day offsite meeting at an outside venue, such as a community hall, where you could do improv workshops or other fun, team-building activities together.

When Josee made the team laugh, they shifted from boredom to full engagement with each other. What would happen if you introduced "pylons" in your workplace?

Our Deeper Issues

~ 20 ~

Bullying: Dogs against Cats

When dealing with a bully, be direct and specific and make your expectations clear: bullying is not acceptable in the workplace.

Mitchell and Catherine, our friends and neighbours who own Timothy, the Great Dane, have an agreement with us. We dog-sit for each other whenever we can. This allows us to go away for weekends and sometimes even longer vacations without having to put Josee or Timothy in a kennel. It also means we can relax while we're away, knowing that our dogs are having fun and being spoiled—they get a vacation too.

Last summer, I was at Catherine and Mitchell's home, dog-sitting Timothy and cat-sitting Timmi. My husband, Mark, was out at baseball, so Josee had joined us for the evening. Timmi is a typical Siamese cat in that she has a healthy respect for dogs. She's timid and rarely shows her face when visitors are in the house. It takes time for her to warm up to new people. It was only during my second evening that she showed herself to me.

While Timmi and Timothy co-exist in the same household , Timmi doesn't go into any room while Timothy is there. She respects his space. And up in the third storey, she has a special door that she can use to access the spot where her food is placed. That's her dog-free zone.

As I mentioned in Chapter 2, Timothy and Josee are often rambunctious when they get together. That evening, I was tired and needed to relax, as I'd been going back and forth between Timothy's place and my home office for two days. So I was settling in to watch one of my favourite TV shows, knowing that my work was done for the day and that the dogs were calmed down. Timothy was sleeping to the right of me on the couch, and Josee was lying on the rug, completely relaxed. I was experiencing a feeling of calm relaxation settling over me and was planning to stay put for a few hours, undisturbed.

As I was watching the program, I noticed, out of the corner of my eye, that Timmi was slowly coming up the stairs, thinking it was time for dinner. Apparently, she was under the impression that the room was dog free, since everything was so quiet. I sat there observing and thinking, "This should be interesting." Suddenly, Josee looked up, and I could have sworn I heard her say, "Did I really see *a cat!?* Then, within a half second ... pandemonium! Josee was wide awake and running down the stairs after poor Timmi. Timothy then woke up from his deep sleep and joined Josee in the chase without a second thought.

Needless to say, I had little choice but to follow them as well. Down on the second floor, I could hear scuffling noises coming from one of the bedrooms. When I got there, Timmi was hiding under the bed, and both dogs were sniffing at her with tails at full mast, wagging in excitement. Josee's head was completely under the bed, and her rear end was sticking up as she kept trying to get closer to what she saw as her new playmate. I literally had to call off the dogs. Poor Timmi was so frightened that she stayed under the same bed until Josee went home and Timothy was stowed in his crate for the night.

I think it's fair to say that Timmi innocently entered her usual dog-free space, completely unaware of what was lurking there, and became a victim of mistreatment through no fault of her own. She was simply in the wrong place at the wrong time. This is often true of people who have been bullied. Little needs to be done to provoke the bully, since bullies are often reactive and have little insight into what is actually going on. Bystanders may then get into a state of nervous excitement, and as a result, like Timothy, they may get involved before they realize what they're doing.

How often have you witnessed co-workers jumping on the bandwagon of someone else's issue at work? I think Timothy is not alone in how quickly he became involved, and people will also often leap at the opportunity of experiencing and supporting another person's drama. There can be a pull to become involved as you get sucked into the vortex of the nervous excitement.

I recently heard, on my local radio station, a newspiece that dealt with the issue of new co-workers bonding around complaining about another person or situation. This is a form of pseudo-rapport because you have a common bond of dislike, which creates intensity in the new pseudo-friendship. You believe that you have a common interest and so you start thinking in some of the same ways as each other. The result is that you have a tendency to continue to talk negatively about this person or situation throughout your relationship. After all, this is the basis of your friendship.

When someone vents to you about their irritation with another co-worker, take a time out before you agree fully with their point of view. Ask yourself whether they've arrived at a conclusion that is fair and has been thought out, or is it possible that the person's observations are based on an inaccurate emotional reaction? Consider what the venting person's role may be in the situation. Be careful not to choose sides, as you may inadvertently become involved in an "us-against-them" dilemma. Ask yourself what is driving the thoughts and actions of the person making the complaint. What is motivating them to act in this way?

As a manager or supervisor, staying neutral in a potential conflict at work can be challenging, but it is usually the most appropriate course of action. However, you'll sometimes need to step in, since it's your responsibility to ensure that all staff feel safe in the workplace. The Ontario Ministry of Labour has legislation about how employers need to handle workplace violence and harassment—based on the concept that every working Ontarian should feel confident that they will be safe at work.

Recently, I offered a workshop called "Employee Morale in the Workplace." One of the participants, a supervisor in a grocery chain, shared a story of a person who was bullying the staff and was also aggressive with management. He discussed how his manager had placed this employee in the back room, putting inventory away, thus segregating her from other employees. The supervisor's concern was that other employees had been subjected to the bullying and that it would appear to all that the bully was being rewarded for inappropriate behaviour (as the bully got her preferred work assignment). During the workshop, we talked about how the supervisor was intimidated by the employee's bullying. He left the seminar ready to address the situation directly with his manager and the employee—realizing that he could make the choice not to be intimidated by this person.

Most bullies act the way they do in order to compensate for feelings of inadequacy, fear, and low self-esteem. They are often afraid that others will call their bluff, so they show aggressive behaviours to protect themselves from what they fear most: others getting close to them and realizing that they are not as strong as they appear. When dealing with a bully, be direct and specific, and make your expectations clear. Once the bully realizes that you're willing to address them directly and that you won't run away in fear, they will tend to be more respectful. It's as if they're acting like an out-of-control child who is really seeking strong boundaries.

As a supervisor or manager, it's vital that you address bullying problems effectively, but this is a challenging type of behaviour to confront. First, be sure that you're self-aware, in order to handle the situation in the most appropriate manner and not like the supervisor who was intimidated by his worker. Being self-aware will help you avoid yelling at—or running from— the bully. Feeling fear is normal in dealing with bullies, so let yourself feel the fear, but confront the person anyway.

How to prepare yourself to address a bully:

- What feelings arise for you, just thinking about approaching the bully?
- Have you ever been bullied?
- What supports do you need in your life to work through this situation?
- Does your employer provide training in dealing with bullies? Does your community provide this type of training?
- Were you ever the bully?
- How did you feel as the victim or as the bully?
- What did you need and want when you were the victim? What did you need and want if/when you were the bully?
- If you were a bully in any given situation, reflect back on how you were feeling. What caused you to act that way? What helped you change your behaviour?
- As a victim, what made you vulnerable? Have you addressed this issue?
- Do you have supports in your life to help you deal with the current issue? If you have supports, there will be less risk that you'll be triggered to respond based on past emotions from previous experiences during the confrontation.

Take a deep breath and be clear about what you need and how you wish to be treated. Let the bully know that you, and your team members, will no longer tolerate the way they've been treated and that you deserve respect. Arrange to have your support person available after you meet with the bully, in order to debrief and/or celebrate once you've dealt with the issue.

If you notice that members of your team are forming cliques (producing in-groups and outer groups), find out what's happening within the team. Cliques are great breeding grounds for bullying behaviour. If your team is beginning to divide into camps of different thinking, make sure you create space where the differences can be aired and discussed. Get to the bottom of the issue. Be the best investigator you can be without taking sides.

Help your employees understand each other's viewpoints, values, and needs. The first step is to "call off the dogs" (the bullies or the people most involved in forming cliques), to make sure that everyone feels safe at work. Second, take the time to help your employees understand what is motivating the bully's behaviour at a deeper level. Ask what triggered their behaviour. Were there any major stressors that acted as triggers? When did their behaviour start? Are you dealing with someone who has an addiction problem? If so, take the time to document what is occurring at work. Ask Human Resources to assist you with the company's internal policy regarding addictions. What is available in terms of counselling through your benefits package or do you have an employee assistance program?

If one of your team members is currently experiencing bullying, take them aside and find out what they need to help them become comfortable again. Since they may need a referral to counselling, make sure that you're aware of resources your company can offer them. Also be sure to obtain details about the bullying and offer to help them confront the bully if they so choose. Give the victim solid support and keep checking in with them throughout the process. Help them see the benefits of confronting the bully, such as the resulting feeling of empowerment and setting boundaries with support. Tell them that a bully is often a person with low self-esteem, who engages in the behaviour as a self-protection mechanism.

Even if you and/or the victim confront(s) the bully, the bully may also require counselling—to help them work through their self-esteem issues and to learn more appropriate ways of interacting with co-workers.

As a supervisor or manager, always take steps to address bullying behaviour. Imagine what would have happened to Timmi if I had not taken responsibility for calling off the dogs. Timmi was in a vulnerable place, where she could not protect herself, and it was my responsibility to step in and ensure her safety. You also need to protect victims of bullies and then work on eliminating bullying from your workplace.

~ 21 ~

Burnout

Burnout can be prevented when employees are in an environment where self-care and respect are nurtured.

Josee is teachable. She loves to learn new tricks. Her toy box is a large, oval basket that sits beside our fireplace in the living room. When her toys are all put away, it's brimming over, and when the basket isn't full, the large area rug in our living room is completely covered with dog toys. She takes over the whole room with her things and makes a big mess. Generally, I pick up the toys every evening. But one night, I decided to teach Josee how to pick up her toys, thinking she'd be smart enough to learn to do this herself.

Knowing how dogs learn, I broke the process down into several steps. The first was "Pick Up," an activity she sometimes does well. "Good dog," I said (this being recognition through verbal praise). Next step: "Carry," which she learned when she started carrying her Frisbee to the park. More recognition through verbal praise. Next step: Direct her to the toy box, using "Over Here," a command she also knows well. Verbal praise. "Drop It." (Josee's accustomed to that command too.) Treat. So I knew she'd be able to perform each step, one at a time, but my plan was to work on the command "Put Toys Away," which meant she'd do all the clean-up herself with no intervening prompts.

I started the first training session at about nine o'clock one evening. Josee often wanders off to her crate for the night at about this time— and gets out of bed only if someone decides to give her a snack that looks appealing to her. We were both tired when I started to teach Josee. Mark was sitting in his chair watching TV and observing our lesson at the same time.

I stood over the toy-covered rug, pointing to her stuffed rabbit, and said, "Get it." Josee successfully picked up the rabbit. I then walked over to the toy box and said, "Here." Josee responded by carrying the rabbit over to the basket. "Drop it," I said, and she dropped the stuffed toy into the basket. "Good Dog!"

I repeated the process for her stuffed gorilla. But this time, when I said, "Get it," she picked it up thinking we were going to play with it. "That's okay," I thought. "She's done as asked." "Good girl," I said, and then, "Over here." She brought the gorilla over to me. But when I said, "Drop it," she dropped it just beside the basket. "Okay," I said to myself, "she's done most of the activity, and I can finesse it with her later."

We continued the routine for a couple more toys. By this time, I was feeling quite positive, thinking about how I might be able to get her to do this every evening before her bedtime. Then I'd get to wake up to a clean living room every morning. But as this thought was crossing my mind, Josee started to lose interest and then became completely bored. I decided to up the ante and get treats to reinforce her learning. That made her go from slightly disinterested to completely distracted, because she was now motivated only by the treats and no longer had any interest in the task at hand. Being stubborn, I continued to work with Josee, determined to teach her this routine. But before long, I recognized that she was burned out for the evening and had no interest at all in the proceedings. I resolved to come back to the training task another day, when Josee was less tired, since her fatigue level and the repetitive nature of learning the trick had burned her out.

OUR DEEPER ISSUES ~ Burnout

At work, people also burn out—because of stress and sometimes because of the repetitive nature of the tasks they're required to do. And when jobs are predominantly outside an individual's areas of personal interest, the employee can succumb to exhaustion. In summary, burnout happens when a worker is stressed, bored, and exhausted by the day-to-day grind of their jobs. Employees can also burn out as a result of feeling unsupported when stressful events occur.

As a supervisor or manager, it's your responsibility to create a supportive workplace, where individuals feel valued for their work and are given appropriate assignments that line up with their abilities. Make sure that you're fair in your dealings with all staff members. Put a solid recognition plan in place and actualize it. Set realistic expectations. If you're short staffed, don't assume that one person can take over all the other tasks of another team member. If an individual is taking on extra tasks, how might you recognize that? Be sure that you're clear in your expectations and that you allow staff to have maximum control over the way they complete their tasks. Be careful not to micromanage; instead, let your workers know that you're there to support them and that they should feel free to seek you out if they're having difficulty with any part of their job.

Ensure that your team is having fun even when they're working hard. As suggested in Chapters 11 and 13, help your employees explore the link between their personal values and the values of the company. If there is a high level of inconsistency between these value sets, the employee who holds the different beliefs will find it stressful to go against their personal convictions in order to meet the demands of the job. It may be best to support that worker to seek alternative employment and give them time to do so.

Lorraine experienced burnout while working in a very busy emergency veterinary clinic. She was in an environment of high expectations and high demand. Employees were given little power or influence over how they did their jobs, and given that they were working with vulnerable animals and their owners, there were many crises in their day. The clinic was also set up in such a way that employees would be expected to work through their breaks. Eventually, Lorraine became completely exhausted and lost her positivity. She was once confronted by management because she'd told a client that she was on lunch and would get back to her after lunch. She'd had a very busy, stressful morning with no break and needed some down time. On that day and at other times, she felt that nothing she did was good enough for her employer.

On top of all this, co-workers were quick to challenge each other if they perceived that another employee was not acting appropriately. But they were not willing to praise each other for a job well done. I believe they really couldn't be emotionally supportive of each other because they were all so highly stressed.

When Lorraine experienced stress exhaustion, no one noticed that it was burnout. She was feeling negative and critical of her work, her co-workers, and even her clients. Instead of getting support at work, she was frequently confronted by fellow staff members. Management supported this negative behaviour by having her direct supervisor hold a meeting with Lorraine and the entire team. During this 40-minute event, Lorraine was told how difficult she was to deal with and how she was causing other workers to stay away from work. She had no allies in the meeting. After the meeting, she asked the least confrontational team member whether she had distorted the content of the meeting, because she remembered getting only one piece of positive feedback. That team member said that Lorraine understood correctly. She'd received only one positive comment. Lorraine's supervisor sat by and did nothing to stop this attack on her. He didn't even ask anyone else in the meeting whether they had played any role in what had occurred. It seemed that he was blaming Lorraine for all the negative dynamics on the team.

She finished her day of work in a robotic state. When she went home that evening, she was in tears and hated herself. She seriously thought about suicide because she felt she was such a horrible person to have caused others so much pain and didn't deserve to live any longer.

A few weeks later, Lorraine went to work in the morning and fell into tears. She couldn't stop crying and so couldn't be with any patients. A kind co-worker suggested she go to her family doctor and take time off work. Finally, someone realized she was burned out. The next day, she was in her doctor's office being given an antidepressant because at that point, given the lack of support at work, she was in a significant depression. She was off work for about five weeks until the antidepressant took effect.

What does burnout feel like? If you are the individual suffering from burnout, you may experience some of the following symptoms:

- exhaustion and possibly sleeplessness
- strong feelings of boredom and lack of energy
- complete lack of motivation
- lack of concern about your appearance
- being uncharacteristically late with deadlines
- feeling disinterested in life activities
- being short with key people in your life, since you are easily frustrated
- being critical and cynical about work
- losing interest in hobbies and personal interests
- losing the sense of job satisfaction you once experienced
- getting headaches, back aches, stomach problems, or other physical symptoms
- drinking alcohol and/or eating more to cope with your exhaustion

If you are supervising someone who is experiencing burnout or stress exhaustion—or if you're their co-worker—you may notice that the person has a shortened attention span and fails to complete tasks and/or does not perform them to their normal standard. Some individuals who are in this state of stressed fatigue may appear tired, less patient than usual, a bit jumpy, stressed, and bored. They may seem negative in general and may be critical of the workplace and of others.

As a supervisor or manager, it's important to be familiar with the symptoms of burnout. If you suspect one of your team members is undergoing stress exhaustion, take them aside and share your concern for them. Be supportive. Ask them whether they're experiencing the symptoms listed above. Help them identify people or groups in their lives who will listen and give support. Find out about any employee assistance program that offers counselling and any company benefits that would cover a portion of counselling costs. Also be aware of the types of counselling that are covered by your company's plan so that you can provide your employee with this information. A good counsellor can help the individual understand the underlying factors that caused the burnout, and this is essential for recovery.

Ask your burned-out employee about job satisfaction. If it is lacking, ask them what they believe has caused this. Like Josee, they could be bored because of the repetitiveness of their work. Perhaps their work is no longer challenging or meaningful for them. If they're having difficulty sleeping, find out whether you can flex their schedule so they can come in later and leave later in the day. Ask them what they need and what is missing for them in their workplace. Help co-create a plan that will help your team member decrease their stress and increase their job satisfaction. Stress has a physical effect, as well as an emotional/psychological effect, so your employee may need to take a stress leave in order to help their body recover.

When a worker comes back from a stress leave, be supportive and also have your other team members check in with the returning worker. In this way, the person will know that they have people who care about their well-being. Set up a weekly meeting with your worker, so you can find out how they are doing and what you can both do to make for a good transition back to normal work.

Burnout happens. But as a supervisor or manager, you can help prevent burnout or reduce its impact. For instance, make sure that your work environment is based on positive feedback, respect, and cooperation. Be on the lookout for signs of burnout, and if an employee is in this situation, give them full support as soon as you notice the problem. This will help prevent further distress, and it will also show all team members that you're trustworthy. And they'll then be more comfortable in seeking you out for support during stressful periods. Be the best role model you can be.

~ 22 ~

Mental Illness in the Workplace

The demands and stress of today's working world
have led to increased occurrences of mental illness.

Shortly after Mark and I were married, we decided to get our first dog. That was Duke, the black Lab cross I first mentioned back in Chapter 1. As my husband and I were both commuting to and from work and putting in long hours, Duke was spending a great deal of time alone in the house. So we decided we should find another dog to keep him company.

I responded to an ad at our local grocery store that said, "Dog for free—German Shepherd Collie X." Then off we went to a farm outside of town, where we were greeted by about 20 cats, 5 dogs, and the kind woman who was taking care of the whole swarm. Then Tippy, the dog from the ad, appeared. She noticed me right away and started wagging—from her head to her tail. Her entire body was wagging. She was a medium-sized dog—mostly tan coloured, with a black "saddle" marking on her back. As I bent down to greet her, she came right up to me on cue as if she'd been taught how to capture a person's heart in one easy step. She put her beautiful face right up beside my cheek and kissed me. I melted inside. It was instant love. I looked up at Mark and said, "Let's take her." He nodded.

We chatted with the farm woman for a few moments, to find out more about Tippy. She'd been given that name because she had white on the tips of her paws. She'd been found abandoned on another property. I'm not sure how much time she'd spent alone in the house before she was discovered by this kind woman and taken in, but she'd definitely spent some time on her own. On the way home, we decided to rename her Tiffy.

Soon after Duke and Tiffy met, they became good friends, so we felt optimistic that we'd made a good decision. When we took them for walks together, they were both happy. And on weekends, we all had a good time together, the dogs playing and Mark and I enjoying the entertainment. Then Monday would come, and we'd have to get to work. We put the two pets in our newly renovated mud room. That was where Duke had always stayed while we were at work.

When I came back from work the first Monday, Duke and Tiffy were right there, but Tiffy had done significant damage to the mudroom. We hoped that as the weeks went by, she'd get comfortable and stop the behaviour. But no, it didn't stop. And one day, she clawed right through the walls, tearing out the insulation and our newly installed vinyl floor. We knew we were in trouble and needed help. We called the place where we'd previously boarded Duke.

Fortunately, the owner of the kennel was a dog behaviourist, who was willing to have us come in for an appointment. When we described Tiffy's antics, he told us that she had severe separation anxiety. Whenever we left, she would panic, thinking we'd never return. Our kennel owner helped us to create a behaviour modification program for her. We were not to talk to her, pet her, or acknowledge her for 30 minutes after we returned home each day. The plan was to do this for six weeks to help her become more secure in herself and less dependent on us humans. This was torture for Mark and me, as we are both dog lovers who enjoy contact with our dogs. We also gave up interacting with Duke for 30 minutes after our daily return, since we felt we couldn't acknowledge him without also acknowledging Tiffy.

Despite these challenges, we did our best to follow the plan, knowing that Tiffy needed to become comfortable with herself if this problem was going to go away. And if this plan didn't work, we felt we might have to put our beautiful new dog down. We lasted a bit more than a week, ignoring them as we'd been instructed. We noticed that Tiffy's behaviour had already improved, so we fixed up the destroyed parts of our mudroom. Over a period of weeks, Tiffy learned to stay calm when we left her with Duke for the day. From time to time, she'd have a bit of a relapse, and she might chew on a book or something else that had been left in the mudroom by mistake. But eventually, she became almost completely calm, and her separation anxiety disappeared.

Like Tiffy, individuals at work may be suffering from undiagnosed conditions that need to be treated. Had we ignored Tiffy's struggles, she would not have received the treatment she so badly needed. It was simply a matter of finding the right supports for her so she could get relief from this anxiety and become the dog she was destined to be. Tiffy lived successfully with us for over 15 years.

It's estimated that one in five adults in Canada suffers from a mental illness during their lifetime. So it's possible that one of your employees has had, or will have, a mental struggle when working for you. As a supervisor or manager, you can play an important role in supporting team members who have mental health issues. By educating yourself about the signs and symptoms, you can help your staff by supporting their needs, and you may play an instrumental role in identifying their issues for them.

Despite advances in knowledge and attitudes about mental illness, it still carries a stigma. Many people live in secret shame because they believe that others will see them as flawed and unworthy if they reveal any mental health problems they are dealing with. They're also afraid of being mistreated or dismissed if they share their situation at work—even with a supervisor or manager. But most people with mental health challenges are treatable, and with the correct remedies, will lead lives that are just as productive as those of their co-workers.

Every year, employers lose money to mental illness because of absenteeism and reduced productivity. Much of this loss could be prevented through education about mental health, greater understanding of the issues, and the provision of appropriate supports. As a supervisor or manager, it is vital that you know the signs and symptoms of mental illness. If you suspect that one of your team members has an issue and if you have a solid rapport with your employees, you are in a place of influence. You could ask a staff member who you think is grappling with a mental illness to check out a website like the Canadian Mental Health Association (CMHA). CMHA is responsible for education and advocacy for individuals with mental health challenges and for the families that support them. In addition to providing helpful resources, they are available to answer questions.

Some symptoms that are common to a number of mental illnesses include the following:

- confused thinking
- prolonged sadness or irritability
- mood swings
- excessive fear or worry
- social withdrawal
- dramatic changes in sleep and eating
- strong feelings of anger
- seeing or hearing things that are not there
- inability to cope with daily problems and activities
- denial of obvious problems
- unexplained physical problems
- thoughts of suicide
- abuse of alcohol and drugs

Employees with mental health challenges will often demonstrate an ongoing pattern of behaviour that signifies their illness. These symptoms may show up in the workplace as:

- consistent lateness and absences from work
- low morale
- lack of cooperation or inability to work with colleagues
- decreased productivity
- increased accidents
- frequent complaints about fatigue
- unexplained pain
- problems with concentration (including problems with making decisions and/or remembering)
- making excuses for missed deadlines and poor work
- decreased interest in, or involvement with, their work

If you notice any of the patterns of behaviour listed above, it will be wise to discuss them with the employee. Make sure that you're non-judgemental and supportive of the individual. Before talking with your team member, it can be helpful to speak with Human Resources, to find out what supports are available for the individual and for you. Also contact the CMHA or a mental health agency in your community to obtain information about supports and other resources they can provide for you and for the employee. You can also ask for tips on how to best address the specific symptoms with your employee.

Remember that the majority of individuals with mental illness live productive lives once they receive the appropriate treatment. Just like a physical sickness, mental illness requires the right treatment and consistent, compassionate support. Rather than reprimanding the team member for late work, for instance, deal with the issue in a supportive way. Begin the process by asking your employee how they are feeling lately. Do they have any concerns? Then, in a supportive and encouraging manner, outline your specific concerns for them. Ask them again if they're aware of the issues you've mentioned. Ensure that you inform them that mental illness is an *illness*, not a character weakness. If you are met with denial, consider this to be potential confirmation that you may be dealing with a mental health challenge.

It may be helpful to share any personal experience that you've had with similar issues. Have you or has someone in your life suffered from a mental illness such as depression or bipolar disorder? Describe how they changed when they brought appropriate supports into their lives. Or tell your employee how you wish they could have received the treatment they needed to have a better quality of life. This can help reduce the stigma that your employee may have attached to their own mental health issue.

Have up-to-date pamphlets available to give to the team member who is suffering from the illness. Review what supports your employer offers (such as employee assistance programs for counselling and/or funding that your company makes available for counselling). It's important for you to be aware of this information yourself, since the employee may not be in a position to seek out or remember resources like these. Encourage your team member to bring more support into their lives. You may also need to build some flexibility into your policies to accommodate your employee's needs, just as you would for someone with a physical limitation.

Being supportive of an employee who is struggling with a mental health challenge will prevent unnecessary absenteeism and team struggles. Other team members may also need education about mental illness to help support the individual. Most communities have mental health advocacy agencies that will offer workshops to help others understand mental illness.

By showing compassion and understanding and by offering support, you will help your employee experience less shame about their illness. This, in turn, will encourage them to seek the supports they need. In all your interactions with the employee and with other team members, make sure that you maintain confidentiality. That is, do not share any information about the person's illness with your team unless the individual gives you permission to do so. While mental illness is no different than physical illness, because of the stigma, you will need to be extra cautious in handling inquiries about their absence. You'll need to answer with the utmost care, to ensure that your employee's personal information is kept private and is respected.

Occasionally, you may encounter a situation where an employee's illness creates a behaviour that impacts the team directly. For example, if a person is suffering from psychosis (loss of contact with reality— often with hallucinations or delusions), they may make inappropriate comments, or their behaviour may be uncharacteristically angry or loud. If this happens, you will need to invite the individual into a conference room or somewhere where they have space and are not on display. Contact your Human Resources Department and manager for help in escorting the employee from the workplace and to ensure followup with a doctor. In severe cases, it may be necessary to involve an ambulance or the police to ensure everyone's safety. Once the crisis is over, gather the team for a short debrief, so staff can talk about their experience in a supportive environment.

Remember that, like Tiffy, most individuals with mental health challenges go on to live healthy, productive lives and are good workers when they receive the treatment they need.

~ 23 ~

Employees' Hunches

*If you're not open with your employees, they'll use their intuition
and past life experiences to draw conclusions about your
behaviour—whether those conclusions are accurate or not.*

A few months ago, I went to Toronto and stayed overnight at the home of my good friend Jill. When we got up in the morning, we had breakfast together and then decided to work on different floors of the house. That way, we'd focus and get our work done. Jill has an incredibly cute dog named Dexter. He's a Polish Sheepdog cross with long, white fur and grey blotches—and deep, dark brown eyes that draw you in. He tends to bark when conversations are happening, but otherwise, he's a calm, quiet dog.

While we were working away, Dexter was sleeping peacefully in his normal spot, in the hallway near the front door. After a while, I felt as if I needed my daily dog walk, and I thought to myself, "Maybe I should take Dexter for a walk." Right then, Dexter woke up and walked over to me as if he was saying, "I'm in. Let's go!" But Jill was on a phone call and I didn't want to bother her to let her know we were going out, so I kept working. Dexter resumed his nap in the front hallway.

About an hour later, the same idea came to my mind. "I really need some exercise," I thought. "And I could take Dexter with me." Again,

Dexter rose from his comfy slumber and walked over to me. At the same time, a colleague called me on Skype to chat about some business-related items and, again, I re-engaged in my work. Dexter calmly walked back to his esteemed resting spot.

After my Skype call, I thought, again, "I should take Dexter for a walk." Like clockwork, Jill's pooch got up and came over to me. By this time, Jill was off the phone, so I told her we were going off for a stroll, and Dexter and I headed out for our refreshing and much-needed exercise.

Dexter had reacted to my thoughts three times, but otherwise, he'd had no interaction with me. Clearly, he had some intuition about what I was thinking that morning. And by responding to his intuition, he finally managed to get a relaxing walk. I truly felt he was reading my mind.

Like Dexter, Josee has always been in tune with me and can tell when I'm thinking about going for a walk. When she and I were in dog training, we got report cards that usually said, "Great team" because we worked together so well. She has a way of anticipating my next move—as if she has a sixth sense about me. She knows how to read my behaviour and knows when I'm not my normal, happy self. Like Dexter, she seems to have the ability to read my mind.

She can definitely tell whether I'm experiencing true emotion or not. When I'm out of sorts, she tends to check in with me as if she's saying, "Are you okay? If there's anything I can do to support you, just let me know." At times, Mark and I have been joking around and I would pretend he was hurting me. Josee would then come and play with us. She can tell the difference between sincere and false emotion. Whenever I've been really hurt, she runs over to me to make sure I'm okay. On occasions like this, she approaches more gently than she usually does, to make sure she doesn't injure me more.

Like Josee and Dexter, team members will try to read their manager or supervisor. Many will be able to pick up on nuances that tell them whether you're revealing the truth or not. Others will draw conclusions based on their life experiences. And your team members will have discussions based on their sixth sense about you. They will read into your behaviour and make assessments about what is happening whether their observations are accurate or not.

John worked as a probation officer and went through a period of time when his area manager appeared to be ignoring him. Using what he thought was his intuitive sense, John began creating reasons why she would do so. He proposed to himself that she was upset with him, and he spent time trying to understand what was happening. But he never guessed accurately. When his manager did speak with John, she told him that she'd been avoiding him because she was told by her superiors to lay him off when she next spoke with him. The provincial budget that had just been passed resulted in all contract employees in the Ministry being laid off. John was one of those contract employees.

John thought his area manager was upset with him and spent time trying to understand what he'd done to make her react that way. Instead, he'd done such a good job that she was trying to keep him on her team as long as possible.

When your team members realize that you're not being congruent with your normal behaviour, they'll know that something is wrong. Then they'll create their own stories or versions of events. The mind reading that they do may or may not be accurate. The stories they create and share with others may damage your reputation.

For example, Sarah was a manager in a deli. She was generally honest, straightforward, and fun to work with. After a phone call with the franchise owner, however, she came out of her office looking stressed and pale. She had just learned that the franchises had been bought out by a competitor and the future of the store was unknown. The owner had instructed her to keep this information confidential. Wanting to respect her employer's wishes, as well as wanting to prevent stressing her employees, she kept this information to herself.

Unfortunately, one of her employees, June, was intuitive and picked up on the situation. June asked to speak with Sarah and mentioned she had had a dream the night before that the deli was going to be closed within three months. Sarah did not confirm June's suspicions. June felt that Sarah was being dishonest or avoiding something (Sarah had avoided eye contact during the discussion and her body language was not consistent with her words).

As in the case of Sarah and the deli, some of your employees may be naturally intuitive, and when difficulties make you stressed or result in uncharacteristic behaviour on your part, they may not understand why you're acting the way you are. If you do not tell the truth or are inconsistent with your normal behaviour, they'll pick that up, and they may begin to mistrust you and your statements. They may even lose respect for you. All of these things will, of course, have a negative effect on team functioning.

June shared her intuition about the store closing with her team members. She also sensed that Sarah was holding information back and spoke with her co-workers about the change in Sarah's demeanour. As a result, her fellow employees began to feel insecure and worried about their future. Sarah then spoke with the owner, and they agreed to tell the staff that some franchises had been purchased by a new owner and that they would keep the staff informed about any further developments. When Sarah was honest with the team, they were less suspicious of her and felt they could trust her again. The atmosphere in the deli became more relaxed.

In a variation of the deli example, an intuitive employee may approach you with their concerns, and you may be inclined to describe your situation only to this person. This will result in a scenario where some employees have the information and others don't, thus potentially creating a division within the team. Make sure you don't do this! In order to maintain trust, share information with all team members at the same time.

Employees respect supervisors and managers who are direct, honest, transparent, and consistent. The gossip that can occur as a result of inconsistent supervisory behaviour will steal time away from the task at hand—and it may create a divide in the team if different employees believe they know the cause of the behaviour, while everyone else is wrong. Often, the stories your employees create will be more colourful than what is really happening. Whatever the gossip may be, as it continues, the team's trust in the supervisor or manager will keep on decreasing.

If you're under a great deal of stress, let your team know that too. It may not be appropriate to share all the details, but simply by letting your employees know where you're really at, you'll be helping them feel more secure. A side benefit of being forthright about your stress is that your team will often give you space and time if they know you require it. If you're having a bad day and are short on patience, you may choose to let them know that as well. If you are self-aware and transparent about your stituation, your team will have the opportunity to support you. You'll also be a good role model, encouraging team members to be open with you and each other. Of course, if your transparency turns into making constant excuses for being impatient or late, you won't be instilling trust. Your staff will start thinking you're "crying wolf" and then won't be as sympathetic if you really are in a crisis.

Several years ago, a celebrity's son died of a drug overdose. The celebrity then held a press conference that was broadcast on the evening news, to reveal the fact that his son had had a drug problem and had overdosed. By telling the truth, he took all the negative power away from the press. They could not embellish his story, as the truth was out. Hollywood celebrities often do the opposite. They try to hide their problems, and this approach only makes the media more curious and motivated to get to the bottom of the situation. As a supervisor or manager, it's better to take the approach of the celebrity whose son died. Be honest and transparent whenever possible. Don't give your staff reason to invent stories.

Your openness with your staff will create a trusting environment. Team members will be secure in the knowledge that you will readily share any difficult news that they should know about. Since they'll have the necessary facts at hand, they'll no longer need to wonder about "what if" scenarios. They'll be able to focus on their work, knowing that you'll keep them informed of any decisions being made at different levels of the organization, and you'll communicate any other details to them as needed.

I can't fool Josee, since she can always read me. And you can't keep important information away from your employees without triggering curiosity, speculation, and gossip. As always, honesty is the best policy—combined with good judgement about what your team members really need to know.

~ 24 ~

Manager's Intuition

Learn to understand and use your intuition.
Then you'll make better decisions and have greater success.

Josee isn't the only one with a sixth sense. People have it too, though we sometimes don't use it. I've experienced many intuitive insights in my life, and I'm sure most of us have, to different degrees. These are sometimes referred to as "gut feelings" or "hunches." But I've also had times when I had a sense that something was going to happen and that very thing did happen shortly afterwards. It's as if a quiet voice in my head would say something—like "Take your umbrella today" or, at times, something more important. So from experience, I've learned to listen to this inner voice as part of my decision-making process.

Now, many of you may be questioning what intuition really has to do with supervising or managing a team. Some of you may not even feel there is such a thing as intuition or sixth sense. For many, intuition is not a valid concept. For example, I recently had a conversation with a colleague about intuition, and he feels that it's just the ability to absorb concepts and ideas quickly. He doesn't believe that anyone has a sense of inner knowing. But in my experience and in the experience of many, gut feelings also come into play, and for some, there's also that sixth sense that helps guide us into better choices.

A friend was making a decision about whether to accept a job offer that would require her to move provinces. She was very close to family and was concerned about how much she would miss her little nieces and nephews, though she was excited about the career opportunity. While reviewing her decision, she first considered the pros and cons. Then she took a few quiet moments to check in with herself. As she considered accepting the position, she felt a sense of openness and happiness in her body. Then she thought about rejecting the offer and felt a sense of tension in her torso. As a result of all the factors, she made the decision to accept the opportunity. She has been very successful in her career as a result of following her "inner sense" in this decision.

Josee and I now have such a strong bond that I know her and her behaviour very well. For instance, I often get a sense of whether we should go to the park or not. Sometimes I listen to my inner voice and sometimes I ignore it. Generally, when I discount it, I realize afterwards that I should have listened.

Here's an example. Josee has had a number of challenges because of her dominant behaviour, and she's also experienced other dogs that have been dominant and close to aggressive. One day, when Mark, Josee, and I were on our walk, we went to the old gravel pit. That week, there had been a lot of rain, so the ditches and streams were full of water. As we walked along the gravel roadway, we noticed three dogs playing in the water. Needless to say, Josee was quick to run over and join them. I watched from the old gravel road as two of the dogs started jumping and running circles around Josee. There was something odd about their behaviour that I couldn't articulate.

I had a gut feeling that I should remove Josee from the situation, but I saw that she was having a lot of fun and overrode my intuitive sense. So Mark and I let her keep on playing in the water. After a while, two of the dogs kept surrounding Josee almost as if they were challenging her—it was the beginning of aggressive pack behaviour.

The fourth dog was a Labradoodle who was nipping at Josee's rear end. I realized my gut instinct had been right on and called Josee to come to me. Josee was obedient and ran out of the water towards me.

Unfortunately, the Labradoodle followed Josee and kept on biting at her rear end. I don't know about you, but if someone were to nip at me constantly for five minutes or so, I'd lose my cool. Josee lost hers and turned and started to fight with her pursuer. Mark had to separate the two canines.

In retrospect, I realized that the first two dogs, who were circling Josee, were acting like a small pack of coyotes. They were isolating their prey. While they never actually attacked Josee, their energy was enough to get Josee and the other dog going and to heighten their survival instincts. I believe this isolation tactic led to the stress that caused Josee and the Labradoodle to become unbalanced and then start fighting.

We all have gut instincts and intuition that can provide us with insights that can improve our decisions and make our days go better. So it's important to learn to listen to that "inner voice." When you come to understand your sixth sense, you'll be able to use this information to help make decisions, deal with potential problems before they erupt, and generally feel more connected within yourself and with your team members. I believe intuition helps us find more pieces of data to improve our decision making in our daily lives at work and at home.

At work, following our hunches can help provide solutions that might not ordinarily be thought of. As a therapist, I used my intuition on almost a daily basis. I would be drawn to ask questions of my clients that would help them understand their situation at a deeper level. Sometimes the questions I asked didn't seem to be the next logical step, but as I grew to understand my sixth sense more, I would trust it and go forward. Many of my clients told me that I'd made a great difference in their lives, and I believe this was partly because I used my intuition.

Over the years, I've also learned to develop my sixth sense—and have taken courses to work on it. Initially, I didn't realize what was happening to me. I would hear quiet whispers and ignore them, wondering if I was losing my mind. These whispers come to me as thoughts so distinct and relevant to my situation that it's as if I'm actually hearing them. While attending a course, I learned that intuition or sixth sense existed and that was what I had been experiencing. I did different exercises to help me get in touch with my inner sensing, so I'm now able to understand whether something I perceive is based on my intuition, my emotions, or my thoughts. Despite this awareness, I still have a tendency to question my intuition out of my fear of not wanting to make a mistake.

The first step was realizing that something like this exists. The next step was learning to listen for it and not squelch it. Learning to pay attention to your inner sense is about getting quiet within yourself and understanding how you feel in your body about a situation. (You may hear a quiet inner voice—though, for some, this may not happen). As you're making decisions, check how your body feels. Do you feel drawn to move towards a situation or are you repelled by it? Scan your body from time to time throughout the day.

To scan your body, sit quietly with your feet flat on the floor. Then notice any sensations in your head, your torso, your stomach, your back, etc. These sensations may be tightness, a void, discomfort, or other such feelings (and they are different from everyday pains or tightness that you experience physically). Pay attention to any sensations you notice as you ponder your decision. Also notice whether you can hear any "quiet whispers" or other thoughts that stand out and are relevant to your context. Learn to check in with yourself.

As you hear what I call the little whispers or inner thoughts, listen to them. In the same way, listen to physical sensations, or hunches like "Something tells me this is not a good path to follow." It may be helpful to keep a record of these sensations and messages in a journal. Jot down what you sensed might happen, along with the actual outcome. This will help you become clear about whether a given hunch or sense was actually your intuition or wishful thinking or fear of something. Start to notice how the thoughts sound different or where you feel specific sensations in your body. As you practise, you will gain clarity about what you are experiencing.

You can start out with seeking really simple insights, such as sensing where you might park in a parking lot and following that inner thought. Play with it and take safe risks with it. Begin to notice whether these inner thoughts and sensations are accurate. Get to know that "inner voice" intimately so that when you have a sense that you should or should not do something at work or in other contexts, you'll know whether that sense is from your inner voice or not.

As always, when you are getting in deeper touch with yourself, take some quiet time to reflect and understand this inner resource on your own, at home. Get to know what your inner voice felt like or sounded like when decisions you've made based on that inner voice have had the best outcome. Also ask yourself, "What are my emotions and thoughts about this decision?" This will help you clarify the difference between a regular thought and an inner knowing. The same is true when sensing something within your body. Is this an emotion or an inner sensing?

How do you deal with things if you do get a sense of inner knowing about a situation at work? You may decide to wait until another day before you bring up an issue with a worker based on a hunch. In this case, just make sure you're not avoiding a potentially uncomfortable situation that would be best handled the same day. Make sure, too, that the sense you got was really based on your intuition and not just on your emotions or thoughts about the situation.

Once you are clear, then you can share this information, using sentences like "I have a sense that ..." or "I wonder if ..." or even "I am curious what you think about ...." These types of statements give the other person an opportunity to confirm or correct your hunch, because you haven't made the statement as a fact. In this way, you can both save face if your hunch is not completely accurate. You may be surprised how many people ask you, "How did you know?"

Using your inner sense to improve your leadership skills is simply one more tool in your management toolbox. Use it to help make decisions, but consider other facts as well. What other evidence supports or challenges your inner sense? What are the facts as you see them? What might happen if you follow your inner voice? What is the risk of following your inner voice? Then make a fully informed decision based on all the information you have. Continue to pay attention to the accuracy of your inner hunches. Keep a running record of your successes. This will help you evaluate how accurate you are in following your inner sensing.

When you learn to listen to your inner voice, you can use your hunches to help yourself and your team create the best possible plan to deal with a project or with potential setbacks in a project. Long before you reach a critical point, you can be more prepared, and you may even avert a potential crisis.

So next time you're working on a project or making a decision, go to a place of quiet. Allow yourself to become clear about the situation. What are your emotions about the situation? How are you thinking about the circumstances? What does your body feel like? Are there any quiet whispers in your head? Review all this information together to arm yourself to make the best possible decisions and arrive at the best possible solutions in your work.

As you learn to use your intuition in life, you'll be able to give others permission to listen to their own inner guidance system. When this happens, you and your team will begin to be inspired to create dynamic solutions that may be considered out-of-the-box thinking. Our inner guidance can take us to the place where we allow ourselves to take important risks that will help you and your team make better decisions and be more successful.

By not listening to my inner guidance system, I placed Josee in an uncomfortable and potentially dangerous situation. When we do listen to our intuition and our inner voice, we can complete projects more smoothly and bring great benefits to our team members and colleagues.

The Final Bark

As I sit and type this conclusion, Josee is lying quietly beside me as if to show her support for this endeavour. She is affectionate, smart, and full of joy, and she brings love and laughter into my life on a daily basis. I'm grateful to have her in my life.

At times, however, she has made me so frustrated and angry that I've had to put her in her crate so I wouldn't unduly punish her for being a dog. During her first week with us, for example, she used her beautiful white teeth to saw down my prized Japanese maple tree. I had tended to that tree for over three years, and finally, in the fourth spring, it was looking alive. I had won the battle! Then Josee joined our family and I lost my prized tree. The tree was young enough that the stick that was left would have made a lovely switch. Fortunately, I gave myself "time out," left the destroyed tree on the ground, and grabbed Josee by the collar and put her safely in her crate. Then I called my husband for support so I could rant about what had happened. That way, I didn't take my anger out inappropriately on Josee.

Yes, these moments exist when I am so frustrated that I cannot tolerate her. Yet on a daily basis, the rewards of having her in my life have been immeasurable. She has pushed me to be the best I can be. As I witnessed her firm belief in herself, I recognized one of my areas of growth. I took up the challenge and grew into my potential. She has also given me so many stories to share that I credit her, in some ways, for creating this book. My fingers typed the words, but her spirit created the possibilities.

The roller coaster of emotion that I sometimes go through with Josee can also happen in teams. So when your team members really frustrate you, take a time out, do your own work, and be willing to understand your reactions. Then review the relevant chapter in this book and deal with the challenge. And when your team has those great moments of joy, celebrate with them.

We all do our best, though some days it seems that even with all that effort, we still come up short. Generally, though, most people work hard and want the best for the team and the organization. So when you feel that you or another team member has not given enough, remember that to err is human; to forgive, divine. And we are all human.

www.onpurposeconsulting.ca
Email: Sylvia@onpurposeconsulting.ca
Tel#: 519.822.3776

Team Dynamic Solutions

Sylvia Plester-Silk has a unique ability to inspire people to reveal deeper purpose in their lives and work. Combined with her playful and direct approach, Sylvia acts as an important catalyst for engagement and performance improvements as she motivates and guides teams to recognize their most challenging dynamics issues, facilitating swift collaborative resolution.

With 22 years as a Social Worker and Addictions Counsellor including 15 years in private practice as a Therapist, Sylvia's experience and expertise in human behaviour and workplace dynamics provides valuable perspective on what makes teams work.

Driven by her passion for healthy workplaces, Sylvia founded the Team Dynamics Institute, a division of On Purpose Consulting.

✓ If you're looking to surpass your targets and create a highly motivated team, request Sylvia to be your catalyst.
✓ Invite Sylvia to speak at your convention, association or meeting.
✓ To purchase multiple copies for your teams or colleagues please inquire about our volume discounts.
✓ For more information about our programs, contact us or check out our website.